YOUR HYPERACTIVE CHILD

YOUR HYPERACTIVE CHILD

a doctor answers parents' & teachers' questions

Gerald I. Sugarman, M.D. & Margaret N. Stone

Henry Regnery Company
Chicago

Library of Congress Cataloging in Publication Data

Sugarman, Gerald I.   1935-
   Your hyperactive child.

   1. Hyperkinesia.   I. Stone, Margaret N., joint author.   II. Title.
[DNLM: 1. Hyperkinesis—In infancy & childhood—Popular works.
WS350 S947y]
RJ506.H9S83   618.9'28'5   74-6915
ISBN 0-8092-8410-3

To
Sandy
and
Mr. Stone

Credits: Wepman Auditory Discrimination Test courtesy of
Dr. Joseph M. Wepman, Department of Psychology, University of Chicago. Bender-Gestalt Test reproduced by permission of Dr. Lauretta Bender and the American Ortho-
psychiatric Association. Addresses in Appendix A courtesy
of California Association for Neurologically Handicapped
Children, Los Angeles, California and Closer Look, Box
1492, Washington, D.C.

Published by Henry Regnery Company
114 West Illinois Street, Chicago, Illinois 60610
Manufactured in the United States of America
Library of Congress Catalog Card Number: 74-6915
International Standard Book Number: 0-8092-8410-3

Contents

Foreword

This book is different because you, the parents and teachers of hyperactive children, have helped to write it. The questions in this book are the ones you have most often asked about working and living with your hyperactive children. The question-and-answer format of this book makes it easy for you to find specific answers as questions arise, thereby avoiding a laborious search through complicated texts.

As a pediatric neurologist, I have seen over 2,000 hyperactive children in my medical practice, and I have come to recognize the unnecessary despair and guilt with which their parents commonly torture themselves. What made me undertake the task of writing this book was a desire to reassure parents and make them realize that there are constructive, positive steps to be taken in raising hyperactive children. I hope that by providing proper information and guidelines, I will help remove some of the parents' misconceptions so that proper treatment can be given and the children's handicaps can be overcome.

For the teacher, this book offers advice about the learning problems of these children, the techniques used to help solve these problems, and the steps needed to handle various behavioral situations.

This, then, is the purpose of this book: to remove teachers' and parents' anxieties and replace these anxieties with an understanding of the hyperactive syndrome, while suggesting concrete methods for dealing with the children who have it. If these goals are met, these children will no longer be the "lost children" of the past. Instead, they will be able to take their place in society as useful productive citizens.

Gerald I. Sugarman

Acknowledgments

We wish to thank all those parents and teachers who inspired this work by their thoughtful questions. In particular we would like to thank the following parents and professionals who gave us invaluable assistance when they brought their own experiences to this book: Mr. and Mrs. Andretti, Nancy Attaran, M.A., Dora Campbell, Lynn Parkhurst Como, Shirlee Dresser, Elissa Ferraro, Montserrat Fontes, M.A., Nancy Hammond, R.N., Julie Hart, Colleen Hartley, Barbara Henné, Valois Lee, Esther Parkhurst, Dolores M. Pinho, Lucia van Ruiten, M.A.

Chapter 1

The Hyperactive Child

What is a hyperactive child?

We use the word *hyperactive* to describe a child who behaves in a particular way. Adults would say that such a child is "restless," "impulsive," "hard to handle," "has no fear of danger," is "always on the go," "seems to be driven," and, because he lacks self control, he is "without brakes." He has a hard time being accepted by friends, "won't take no for an answer," and he usually "has trouble in school." He tends to be compulsive and aggressive, with a very short attention span and a high-strung temperament. However, these descriptions will not fit every hyperactive child exactly. The range of behavior is wide because there are many degrees of hyperactivity and the severity of the symptoms varies. Also, it is important to realize that hyperactivity is not in itself the *cause* of the child's difficult behavior patterns. *Hyperactivity is only a symptom.*

1

I've often heard teachers refer to problem children as "hyperkinetic." Do hyperactive and hyperkinetic mean the same thing?

Yes. These words are interchangeable. "Hyper" in Greek means "above," "overly," or "more than normal." "Kinetic" is derived from the Greek word "kinesis," meaning "motion." Therefore, *hyperkinetic*, *hyperkinesia*, and *hyperactive* all refer to the most common characteristic of this disorder—too much motion. None of these words should be confused with *hypoactive*, a term often used to describe the behavior of children who are underactive.

What causes hyperactivity?

Most hyperactive behavior is due to a neurological disorder, or an *organic hyperactive brain dysfunction*. The most common cause of this dysfunction is that the baby's brain received insufficient oxygen either before birth, during birth (as the result of a complicated delivery), or later in life as the result of head injury, brain infection, brain tumor, or certain rare diseases. Neurological problems can be inherited or can be aftereffects of such illnesses as pneumonia, mumps, measles, chicken pox, or meningitis. An organic brain dysfunction does not necessarily cause a handicapped life. Through proper treatment and special procedures, other parts of the brain can be trained to take over the duties of the affected parts, allowing the child to lead a normal life. Also, brain dysfunction does not necessarily affect the intelligence centers of the brain. Most hyperactive children are of normal or superior intelligence.

Can an auto accident cause brain dysfunction?

Yes. The temporal lobes of the brain are very sensitive and can be easily injured, especially in an auto collision. Since these temporal lobes control behavior and certain emotions, damaging them may result in psychomotor injury, diminished memory, altered personality, headaches, and abdominal pain. We call this type of injury *cerebral trauma*.

The trauma can also occur as the result of falls or other head injuries. Sometimes the head injury will not show up for months or years after the accident. A chronic subdural hematoma must be ruled out.

Is all hyperactivity caused by neurological disorders?

No. Sometimes hyperactive behavior is the result of emotional disorders. Doctors call this the *functional hyperactive behavior syndrome*. Some psychiatrists think that the emotional cause of the syndrome may be a conflict between the child and his mother. It may also be due to a general anxiety that the child feels and that makes him become nervous, fearful, worried, or apprehensive. General anxiety causes nail biting, finger sucking, nightmares, eczema, bedwetting, and even asthma. Hyperactive behavior may also be a sign of severe emotional disorders such as schizophrenia, although schizophrenia is rare in the overall childhood population. The important thing to remember is that emotional disorders account for only a minority of hyperactive cases. In fact, emotional disorders are more often the result of improper care and misunderstanding of the child who already has neurological problems. This misunderstanding occurs not only in the home but also at school, where teachers may use punitive measures without understanding that the child has a medical problem.

Hyperactivity may also be the result of disturbances to the mother during her pregnancy, among them malnutrition, insufficient prenatal care, or trauma (for example, being beaten by her husband). Other causes for hyperactivity include pain, parasitic infections, anemia, or allergies that the child himself has suffered. In addition, glandular disorders such as an underactive or overactive thyroid or hypoglycemia can produce hyperactive symptoms.

Hypoglycemia? What's that?

Hypoglycemia is *low blood sugar*. This commonly undetected disorder found in adults is also found in newborn in-

fants of diabetic mothers. Diagnosed through a glucose tolerance test, it can be treated with a special diet that is high in
protein and that prohibits sugars, starches, and foods such as
tea and coffee, which stimulate the pancreas, thus producing
more insulin and lowering the blood sugar. Sometimes
amphetamines and ephedrines are also prescribed for obesity.
Symptoms of hypoglycemia include headaches, dizziness, abdominal pain, irritability, mood changes, flushing, increased
respiration, confusion, poor memory, stumbling, ataxia,
drunken gait, coma, and convulsions.

Is hyperactivity an inherited trait?

Possibly, but hyperactivity has many other causes, and the
genetic ones are not yet fully understood. I do suspect that in
some families where there are four to five boys with this
disorder (although this is rare), it could be a sex-linked factor
inherited from the mother. What is important is that neither
parent should feel guilty about the child or blame the other
for any one of his symptoms.

Are there more hyperactive boys than girls?

Yes. Hyperactivity has been observed to affect eight boys to
every one girl. The reason for this phenomenon is not completely understood, but hyperactivity may be a sex-linked
disorder transmitted from mothers to their male offspring. In
other words, the mother may be a carrier for an abnormal
gene that is found on the X chromosome.

Can anything be done during pregnancy to prevent hyperac-
tivity in the unborn child?

Since there is no one cause of the syndrome, we have no one
way to prevent it. However, the best thing a mother can do
is enjoy her pregnancy and carefully follow her doctor's
orders regarding good nutrition, exercise, and emotional
tranquility. For her own health and that of her unborn child,
it is very important that she try to maintain peace of mind.

Is hyperactivity culturally or racially connected?

It is not racially connected, but children from lower socioeconomic income groups do appear to have a higher incidence of the syndrome. This may be due to the greater degree of untreated medical problems—particularly nutritional deficiencies, which appear to be an important factor in hyperactivity—found among these groups. However, no race, culture, or economic class is immune from this disorder.

Under certain circumstances hyperactivity can be the result of the social environment. In a New York study of a densely populated apartment house area, it was found that hyperactive symptoms were being exhibited by children who went directly home from school to their very small apartments, watching TV and remaining indoors until bedtime. Because of a high rate of child molestation on the streets and a lack of open spaces and recreational facilities, the children lacked the necessary outlets for physical energy.

Can a child be hyperactive because there is no father in the home or because the mother has a job away from home?

No. Many "normal" children come from homes where there is no father. However, the father plays a very important role in the structure of all families. He provides the masculine identification that is needed for normal psychosexual growth and development. It is necessary for a boy to have a male model, and he may rebel if masculine influence and discipline are missing. That is why mothers who are alone often find it more difficult to deal with their hyperactive boys. Some psychiatrists believe that hyperactivity is often the result of a psychological disturbance between the personality of the mother and child. In these cases the mother feels that she cannot relate to her child and usually blames herself for the conflict. Actually, it may be the child's own personality disorder that prevents the warmth and bond between them. If there is such a mother-child conflict, it may actually be better if the mother spends some time away from the child.

How common is hyperactivity?

It has been estimated that there is at least one hyperactive child in every classroom in the United States. However, since there are many degrees of hyperactivity, the number is probably much larger because these children have not been diagnosed or recognized as having a medical problem.

Are more adopted children hyperactive than other children?

Yes, there does seem to be a higher frequency of hyperactivity among children who are adopted. Young mothers run a higher risk of difficulty during pregnancy, especially in the emotional stress of an unwanted pregnancy. Or, the hyperactivity may be due to the mother's poor health or lack of prenatal care. The most important thing to remember is that hyperactivity in adopted children is not the fault of the adoptive parents.

How can I tell if my child is hyperactive?

Identification of the syndrome is often difficult. At first you may just notice that as an infant he cries excessively or spends very little time sleeping and that, when he does sleep, he is very restless. As a newborn he may appear to "always be in motion," with a lot of kicking and rolling about. Mothers may feel a lack of the closeness that ordinarily occurs between infant and mother. This feeling may be so extreme that she feels she "can't stand" her own child. Or, the mother may notice that, while other mothers find at least a little time for themselves during the day, her child is so demanding that she doesn't have one free moment.

Later on, the child may become the cause of complaints from neighbors and teachers—perhaps the nursery school requests that his parents remove him because he is "impossible to control." He is usually the child that parents can't take anywhere without his causing some kind of unpleasant or conspicuous scene.

While you may believe him to be merely an overactive

child, your relatives, friends, and other outsiders may comment upon his bizarre behavior. Fortunately, there are teachers and physicians who will be able to recognize that the child's activity level is enough above normal to require medical attention. This is so very important because the sooner the child is diagnosed and treated, the better off he will be. Remember, not all of these behavior patterns may describe your child exactly. There are many degrees of hyperactivity, and each child will vary in his symptoms and impulse control. Each hyperactive child is a unique person with his very own personality.

What's the difference between a hyperactive child and one who is merely overactive?

The most important difference is that the hyperactive child has little or no control over his behavior and does not respond to discipline from his parents and others. He has such difficulty controlling his own emotions and movements that it often appears as if he has another force that is driving his body. By contrast, the overactive child can be controlled and can be reached, although during periods of excitement and stress he, too, may be difficult and very "wound up." It is often hard for parents to distinguish the behavior of the hyperactive child from that of the overactive one. It is the qualified physician who is best equipped to make this diagnosis.

When does hyperactivity usually appear?

The syndrome may be noticeable as early as pregnancy, when the unborn child manifests excessive kicking and a high degree of fetal movement. Sometimes it is very noticeable among newborns who may show signs of colic, vomiting, irritability, and fussiness with long and frequent waking periods. Or, the syndrome may not show up until later in childhood. What is often confusing for parents is the inconsistency of the child's behavior. At times the hyperactivity is quite severe, while at other times it almost seems to go away. It appears especially during stressful periods—for example, during illness and when the child must face new experiences, both pleasant and unpleasant.

Does the hyperactive child have any distinguishing physical characteristics?

No. He looks like any other child of his age. There is nothing physically distinctive about his condition except his unusual degree of activity.

Will our hyperactive child have hyperactive children of his own?

Perhaps. There does seem to be a genetic or family history for this kind of behavior, and many families with hyperactive children have parents and relatives who were also hyperactive. Whether it is the emotional factor or the neurological one that is passed on has not yet been established. However, if hyperactivity is the result of the illness or injury it WILL NOT BE PASSED ON. In any case, the cause should not affect the parent-child relationship.

If we have other children will they be hyperactive too?

Not necessarily. There may be only one child in a family who is affected. More than likely it will be the firstborn child, especially if it is a boy. However, there are some families in which both parents are hyperactive. In such cases, it is likely that more than half of their offspring will be affected.

Will our other children develop the syndrome through contact with our hyperactive child?

No. Hyperactivity is not a contagious disorder. Occasionally other children will copy and mimic hyperactive behavior, but this is not likely to occur often. If this should occur, it will only be temporary.

My husband had the same behavior as a child and outgrew it. Will our child outgrow it?

More than likely, if he follows the same type of hyperactivity as your husband. However, this will depend upon the severity of the disorder, when he developed his symptoms, and how soon treatment begins. *Early treatment is crucial.* Often well-meaning family members will advise, "Leave him alone —he'll outgrow it." But this waiting is trying for all family members and is particularly painful for the parents and affected child. The earlier the child is diagnosed and treated, the better the outcome will be.

How do we know he will outgrow it?

You cannot know certainly. Some hyperactivity, called *developmental hyperactivity*, is a normal variant in a young child of four to five years of age. This form occurs for a period and then gradually subsides. However, if the hyperactivity gets worse with time and there is progressive interference with school learning and peer relationships, the child needs immediate attention.

When does hyperactivity usually stop?

Ordinarily it stops during adolescence. Yet even if the child does outgrow it at this time, if he was not treated at an early age he will be left with emotional, psychological, and achievement problems. In those cases where the behavior syndrome continues into adulthood, it is possible to control it, and these hyperactive adults can lead normal, creative, and productive lives.

I've read that hyperactive children have more lead in their bodies. Is that true?

While some studies have shown that hyperactive children have increased body lead, blood and urine lead levels, the studies are also finding that many children without hyperactivity also have more lead than has been normally suspected. This may be due to our polluted environment. More environmental control measures are being studied at this time.

Do hyperactive children have more allergies than other children?

Yes. It is an interesting association. Many asthmatic children have allergies to foods, trees, dust, grasses, weeds, and pollens, and seem to be more hyperactive at the times their allergies are severe. It has been the observation of allergists that many of their patients are hyperkinetic, and some are referred for more specialized testing. There also seems to be a correlation between the time when hyperactivity diminishes and when allergies are fully controlled on hyposensitization programs and medications by allergists. However, on occasion some of the drugs used in the treatment of asthma cause increased hyperactivity and excitability.

Does bedwetting accompany hyperactivity?

Not usually. For the most part bedwetting is an emotional problem, although it can occasionally be due to infections of the kidneys, bladder, or lower urinary tract. Any emotional disturbance that causes bedwetting may also be associated with hyperactivity, but the two usually do not go together.

Does hyperactivity cause stuttering?

Stuttering is not physically caused by hyperactivity, but it may be the result of the frustrations and pressures that many hyperactive children experience. Stuttering is primarily an emotional disorder.

Does hyperactivity cause poor coordination?

No. Remember, hyperactivity is a symptom, not a cause. Poor coordination is usually associated with neurologically based hyperactivity, which means that gross or fine muscle control is affected as the result of brain dysfunction. The dysfunction can show up in clumsiness, gait disturbances (problems in walking), poor handwriting, poor pencil grasp, poor posture, and difficulty in tying shoes, braiding hair, kicking, hopping, jumping, running, and balancing.

Why does our child get leg pains?

This is a complaint common to all children. With hyperactive children, the pains may be associated with excessive running and jumping. Overuse of the muscles and ligaments may cause pain and tenderness in and around the joints or the muscles themselves. They are not "growing pains," however, and if they do not go away they should be investigated by your physician.

What does it mean if our child gets headaches?

This is also a common symptom in all children. Headaches have many causes, among them visual disturbance, sinus infection, or disorders in the head, neck, or face. If headaches persist, they should be thoroughly evaluated by your physician.

Are headaches more common in the hyperactive child?

No. However, the child's parents and teachers will notice that he will often say, "My head hurts," when he is doing his schoolwork. If this complaint disappears when he is playing, it may mean that the hurting head is an expression of the tension he experiences while learning and his worry about failure in school.

What does it mean if our child complains of headaches and abdominal pains?

This is a frequent association with seizure disorders (called *psychomotor epilepsy* or *abdominal epilepsy*). These symptoms, together with behavior disturbances that are episodic, should be investigated with an electroencephalogram (EEG), especially if the child has no memory of his sudden behavior changes. *These symptoms should not be ignored.*

What do the words "seizure disorder" mean?

A seizure disorder, also referred to as "fits," "spells," "convulsions," or "epilepsy," is caused by some dysfunction in the brain. Seizure disorders can be classified into different kinds. It is easy to recognize the *hard seizure*, called *major motor convulsion*, during which the patient becomes unconscious, bites, and thrashes about with his arms and legs or becomes stiff or limp. However, it is much more difficult to recognize the more subtle types of seizure disorder known as *psychomotor epilepsy*. This type of seizure causes episodic and recurrent headaches, abdominal pains, and sudden changes in behavior for which there may be no memory and no unconsciousness. Other kinds of seizure disorders are called *petit mal*, which is rare, and the not-so-rare *petit-mal variant*, both of which must be diagnosed by the electroencephalogram pattern. Their symptoms are staring, lip smacking, facial movements, and other "spells" that last only a few seconds.

Our hyperactive child doesn't pay attention. Is this because he has a hearing problem?

No. Actually his hearing is probably much better than that of the average child. The reason he doesn't pay attention is not his hearing, but the way in which his brain digests the sounds. He has an *auditory perception problem*, and this makes many parents believe the child has a physical problem with his ears. For the most part, your child is listening but is unable to respond immediately.

Why does our child keep repeating the same questions?

One of the reasons is that with hyperactivity there is constant bombardment of the brain. That is, there are so many stimuli that the brain cannot digest all the information it receives. Also, your child may be repeating questions because he is insecure. Although he may know the answer, he asks it over and over again to be quite certain that he is correct.

Don't be impatient when repeating your answers. I find that it is most effective to have eye contact when you answer questions. Repeat your answers slowly, in simple, exact phrases that your child can understand easily. Be careful in your language and try not to confuse him, since he already has a problem in organization of thought sequences.

My child speaks in a very loud voice. Do all hyperactive children do that?

No, not all. However, those that do speak loudly do so because of poor muscular control of speech modulation, rhythm, and frequency, which may also produce a high-pitched and tense voice. Again, like other acts, speaking loudly is something that he does, not because he wants to, but because he can't help himself.

Why won't he do what he is told?

He can't control his impulses. He is so busy going in all different disorganized directions that he is unable to follow instructions unless they are repeated in very simple terms. It is as if he were receiving red, yellow, and green traffic directions all at the same time.

Why can't he repeat simple tasks that he was once able to do?

It may be that he has actually forgotten the method for solving that particular problem. Also, if there are too many distractions, noises, or other stimulations, he has more difficulty in concentrating. This can cause him to be confused and puzzled and make him give up. All this adds up to a negative pattern of problem solving, bringing about additional frustration.

Why does his behavior fluctuate so much?

The regular upheaval in behavior is typical of hyperactivity and is what makes living with this child so difficult and chaotic for all the family. For, just as soon as you begin to believe you've "got the problem licked," some incident will trigger the entire behavior pattern once again. Generally, it will be a stressful situation that sets him off. The stress can be caused by pleasant as well as unpleasant incidents, such as a big birthday party. Remember that all human behavior fluctuates and that you, as a parent, also have mood changes. If your child's behavior should suddenly swing back and forth from hyperactivity to quietness, however, it may be a sign of an underlying seizure disorder. The more stress placed on a hyperactive child, the more symptoms will be produced. He is placed under stress when he has an infection or illness, when he must meet new situations, or even when he tries to get along with peers. Stress produces feelings of inadequacy and insecurity. Because there are more anxiety-provoking situations in school, there seems to be a correlation between the severity of symptoms that occur and the cycle of the school year. Often there are fewer symptoms during vacation periods.

Why doesn't he ever get tired?

He does, but it may seem to you that he never does because of his boundless energy and movement. After only a brief rest period, the hyperactive child is ready to go again and seems to be fully recharged.

Why does it take him longer to go to sleep?

When the hyperactive child goes to bed, "his battery is still charged"—his brain is still working overtime. Also, the control mechanism does not lend itself to spontaneous relaxation.

Why doesn't he sleep through the night?

Hyperactive children have brains that are constantly stimulated, so that the emotional problems that present themselves during the day must find a way to be expressed and released. This commonly occurs during sleep, which causes him to waken often during the night.

Does the hyperactive child need more sleep than other children?

No. He should receive the normal amount of rest and sleep for children his age. For a young child, this is about twelve hours per day. Later, a child needs about nine or ten hours.

My child sometimes reverts to baby talk and thumbsucking. Why does he do this?

Most hyperactive children do not ordinarily exhibit this type of abnormal behavior. It shows a subconscious desire for the child to go back to a period in his life when he was the most comfortable. This is a symptom of an emotional problem and should be investigated.

Why does he "act up" more with his mother than with his father?

It seems to be easier for most fathers to be disciplinarians than for mothers, since fathers often spend less time at home and can therefore more easily maintain their roles. If the mother has to cope with her hyperactive child 24 hours a day, the child soon becomes fully aware of her fatigue and learns to take advantage of her when he can.

My child seldom comes close to me or lets me hold him. Why is this?

It may be that he does not have the self-control to sit on your lap for even a short length of time. But that does not mean that he does not desire physical contact. In fact, he really needs more love and attention than other children, even though he is unable to request it and has difficulty in controlling his response when he receives it.

It also may be that he senses your discontent and fears

that you will reject him, and so he protects himself by keeping away from you. Another possibility is that there are some children who prefer to initiate expressions of love themselves. In these cases it is best to wait for them to do so and then seize the opportunity to express your own affection in return.

I've seen other hyperactive children who seem overly affectionate. How can you explain that?

As I mentioned before, not all hyperactive children are exactly the same. Their behavior varies as much as in other groups of children. However, when they appear to be overly affectionate it could be an indication of their insecurity, or it might reveal their fear of losing parental love. Overaffection may also serve as an acknowledgment of their rejection by others.

Our child seems so much stronger than his friends. Is he?

No. He only seems to be because of his constant running, climbing, jumping, and general body conditioning. His strength and muscle tone are usually about the same as that of any child of a comparable age.

Why is it so hard for my child to keep friends?

It may be that friends quickly outgrow him because of his immaturity. In other cases, his behavior is hostile, destructive, selfish, and quick-tempered, so his peers prefer avoiding him rather than putting up with him. Unfortunately, the affected child does not realize the cause, and this creates even more frustration and hostility.

Why does he fight so much with other children?

He may be trying to gain attention, trying to prove something to them in order to gain their respect. Often this aggression comes about because he is so frustrated that he has to relieve his hostility and hurt others just to prove his worth.

Does our child realize that he is in constant motion?

This is difficult to assess. Some children are unaware of their behavior and to them it appears completely normal. However, there are some children who consciously use constant motion for attention getting. Although he appears to expend more energy and goes further distances than other children, he actually is not putting on any more mileage. It only appears that way because his static movement is constant and when he moves distances it is in such a disorganized, purposeless fashion.

Why does he have no fear of danger?

There are two reasons. The first one is that he is going so fast he can't stop to anticipate what the consequences of his actions will be. Second, he ignores the normal danger signals because he has no memory of past bad experiences to help him avoid getting hurt again. For these reasons hyperactive children have many accidents.

Why does our child break things so frequently?

One possible reason is his inability to coordinate his movements. On the other hand, his destructiveness may be due to hostility—it is an acting out of his unhappiness in an aggressive way. It may also be an expression of an endless need for love and attention.

Why does he overreact emotionally when being corrected?

He can't help this. It happens because he has poor impulse control, which means he is unable to control his behavior or his abnormal response. This causes him to "overshoot his mark" in his emotional reactions.

Why is he hyperactive at home and not at school?

Perhaps at home he is able to release the frustration and anxiety that is pent up during the school hours, where strict discipline is enforced. Don't forget, it is important for all children to "let off a little steam" at home, and this may be even more important for the hyperactive child.

Why doesn't he understand that he is upsetting his parents, his family, and his teachers?

Maybe he does understand that something is wrong but just doesn't have the control to do anything about it. It is also possible that he doesn't realize what he's doing, or it may be that he actually forgets. With hyperactive children, problems in recent memory are common because there are so many stimuli reaching the brain at one time they cancel each other out, and sometimes cancel out the most important response that is needed. Even if he does become aware of the displeasure he has caused, the child is still unable to control himself. Like an alcoholic, he may promise *never* to do it again, being pure in his intent, only to repeat his performance a short time later. *He cannot help himself.*

How does the hyperactive child feel about himself?

He feels "confused," "dumb," "lost," "unhappy," and "different." He feels guilty about his own behavior because of all the trouble that he causes. He is a child alienated from himself and from others. That is why it is so important to change his ideas about himself by reinforcing your love and acceptance of him and by reassuring him that he is not stupid, that he can learn, and that he *will* learn.

Chapter 2

The Hyperactive Child
in School

Should the hyperactive child attend nursery school?

It depends on the severity of his symptoms. If he is mildly
overactive or mildly hyperactive, nursery school experience
may be helpful for his social adjustment. In general, a good
nursery school offers access to play equipment as well as
other opportunities that most parents are unable to provide.
More important, it gives the opportunity for play and self-
expression under the guidance of a trained teacher who en-
courages the children to get along with each other. However, if your child is severely hyperactive, his condition will
grow worse in a large group situation, which may have disas-
trous effects by creating further episodes of failure for him. If
your child's condition is severe at the nursery school age
level, then this would be the ideal time to begin treatment
for him. It is especially not fair to foist your problem child
onto an unsuspecting teacher, for a child who is "in trouble"
at home will probably be disruptive in school.

Where can we find a good nursery school?

One good place to check is Project Head Start, which has a fine program for four-year-olds. Nursery school facilities can also be found in day care centers, religious schools, public welfare organizations, or other private or nonprofit organizations. If you are fortunate, you may discover a school that provides diagnostic evaluations and behavioral observations.

Do hyperactive children do well in public school?

Not usually. The child will probably have both learning and social problems. Social problems generally arise because it is difficult for the child to pay attention, and as a result he often disrupts the whole classroom. Problems also arise because of his inability to interact well with other children. In addition, he will probably have poor reading and writing skills, and the resulting frustration will only aggravate his social adjustment.

Why is our child failing in school? Are all hyperactive children slow learners?

Whether or not your child is a slow learner depends on whether his hyperactivity is associated with minimal brain damage or mental retardation. Most hyperactive children are of normal or above normal intelligence. However, even if there is no brain damage, their condition may cause them to have special learning difficulties, which can be overcome through special educational therapy.

Hyperactive children with normal and above normal intelligence commonly fail in school. The failure may result from a behavior disturbance, a specific learning problem, or the combination of both of these. Learning problems are the result of perceptual problems, which can be treated and helped. Behavior problems arise because of repeated school failure and poor ego development, which in turn causes hostility, aggression, and rebellion. In spite of all this, your child still wants to learn, and *he can learn* if given the proper setting, opportunity, and understanding.

Why does my child hate school?

He probably doesn't like it because he is not successful there. Not only that, his lack of academic success is noticed by all the other children, causing him to feel worse about himself and decreasing his chances of making social connections with his peers. Further, if he is a disruptive force in the classroom, even his teacher will not be on his side.

Why does the school want him for only part of the day?

Many hyperactive children cannot tolerate full-time schooling because the long hours produce additional fatigue and stress. Because of this, the school may recommend half-day sessions; if the school authorities cannot cope with the problem, they will ask that your child be removed from school.

Should he see the school counselor?

He needs to see *anyone* who will make referrals and recommendations for additional investigation, evaluation, and remediation. This should be done *as soon as possible* when the child has a problem, be it physical, emotional, or educational. Trained personnel at school often are the first to identify the problem child as hyperactive. They do this by testing him and comparing his behavior with that of other children.

My child is on special medication. Can he still go to a public school?

Yes. The school can be allowed to administer medication to such children. Your doctor should send a note, giving the exact dosage and advising when it is to be given and requesting that side effects be noted. This consent should be signed by both the physician and parent. If the school will not agree to such an arrangement, the child may be given long-lasting medication that will hold him through the day.

Can my child stay in a normal classroom or should he be put into a special group?

This depends on the degree of severity of symptoms and your child's response to medication and other forms of therapy. If at all possible, it is always preferable to leave your child in the normal classroom. He can receive extra tutorial help in a private or nonprofit institution or clinic. By placing him in a special classroom, you are only adding to his feelings of being different.

However, the severely hyperactive child should not be in a regular classroom because he disturbs the others and their reaction to him will make him feel more unwanted and rejected. Such a child should be placed in a special classroom, with teachers who understand the medications and who are trained in educational and psychological techniques. The teacher will be able to handle the child and help his progress. If the child has an I.Q. of over 85 and special learning disabilities, an educationally handicapped (EH) classroom situation would be ideal. If your child has normal intelligence and a severe learning problem and you can afford therapy, then a full-time educational therapy school would be ideal, if one is available.

Many children who are retarded and whose I.Q.'s are between 50 and 75 are placed in classrooms for the educable mentally retarded (EMR). If a child's I.Q. is between 25 and 50, then a classroom for the trainable mentally retarded (TMR) would be indicated. Whatever special class you select, you should make a point of visiting it periodically to observe and make certain that it fits your child's needs.

You said most hyperactive children were of normal or above normal intelligence. Why do you suggest putting them in classrooms for children with low I.Q.'s? What is an I.Q., anyway?

I.Q. stands for "intelligence quotient," and it is a score found by dividing the person's chronological age into the mental age and multiplying by 100. For example, if your child is 8 years old (his chronological age), and his mental age on a psychological test such as the Peabody Picture Vocabulary Test or the Stanford-Binet Test is 8 years, then you would arrive at his I.Q. by dividing 8 into 8 and multiplying by 100. His I.Q. would then be 100. The normal I.Q. is from 90-110. The genius has an I.Q. of over 135. If your child has an I.Q. between 50-75, he is considered mildly retarded. If he has between 25-50, he is moderately retarded, and if he is under 25, he is profoundly retarded.

However, parents need to be reassured that, *for children with special educational disabilities and other handicaps, I.Q. has very little meaning.* Unfortunately, most tests and measurements today depend on reading abilities because there is such great emphasis on this skill in our society. If a person is unable to read he's often classified as "retarded," when he may not actually be so. That is why it is so important to recognize reading disabilities as early as possible in order to begin proper remediation. However, the tests do not reflect the intelligence of the disadvantaged child or the child who does not have a real command of standard English.

Performance abilities of the child with learning disabilities will probably be higher than his verbal skills indicate, and the score will not give his true I.Q. For a more accurate evaluation, it is important that the child be given a battery of psychological tests, as well as a complete WISC (Wechsler Intelligence Scale for Children), which will score his verbal and performance tests. (See Appendix D.) Yet even the WISC will not give an exact measure of your child's abilities. We look forward to the time when there will be standardized psychological tests that will be able to determine the exact level of functioning and estimate when that level will be reached.

Should I put my child in a private school?

This is not usually necessary. You pay your taxes, and your child has a right to receive the proper education through the public school system, even if he has a special problem. It's up to you to see that your child is placed in the proper class. If there is a waiting list for special educational classrooms, remain on it until your turn comes, and in the meantime seek other resources. Only if your public school system has no provision for special education programs should you explore the possibilities of private institutions. Usually such institutions offer initial psychological and psychiatric consultation, and educational rehabilitation programs. Although private institutions are generally expensive, there may be some special provisions for those people unable to pay.

Do most public school teachers know about hyperactivity?

Most teachers, unfortunately, do not recognize that hyperactive children have medical problems. It is a real tragedy that the hyperactive child is often simply regarded as "a trouble-maker" or "a problem child." When the teacher punishes the child for his misbehavior, the child's self-image deteriorates even further and his misbehavior only becomes aggravated. School can thus become a painful, destructive experience.

There are some hopeful signs, however. Many states now require teachers to take additional courses in special education. These teachers will be able to recognize the child with a learning disability. Although in the average classroom, the teacher may not have time to give special attention to the child, she can make recommendations to the parents about early evaluation and treatment. Often the school will recommend a teacher called an *educational therapist*.

What is an educational therapist?

An educational therapist is a teacher who is specially trained in methods of teaching the child with specific learning disabilities. The therapist will make use of certain educational testing methods to determine his specific deficits. An extra benefit of educational therapy is that many of the child's emotional problems will be solved through effective teaching and the resulting success experienced by the child.

What does educational testing find out?

Educational testing is given to the child who has learning disabilities to identify his specific learning problems, such as dyslexia and other perceptual difficulties. The tests will find those areas in which the child is developmentally delayed, such as spelling, reading, or mathematics. They will also reveal whether or not the child is retarded. In all cases, the results of the testing are used as a guide for the teacher or therapist in creating a proper remedial program.

How long will educational testing take?

This is dependent upon the child's cooperation, age, and the amount of testing performed. A Bender-Gestalt Test, Draw-a-Person Test, or a reading and spelling test may take less than one hour. Of course, the child must be observed and tested over a longer period of time in order to increase the chances that the results are accurate.

Special Questions Teachers Ask

How can I spot a hyperactive child in my classroom?

In contrast to children with normal behavior, who pay attention, the hyperactive child has a short attention span and disrupts classroom activities. He may have poor coordination. There is constant movement of his body, hands, or legs. He won't stay in his seat and often walks around the room. He also tends to be restless and fidgety, frequently scratching himself, biting his lips, or talking and laughing in a loud voice. When assigned written work, he often will not put his work down on the paper, or he leaves the work unfinished. He has a poor memory, answering a question correctly one day and answering the same question incorrectly the next day. He may not know his left hand from his right hand, and when asked to write may have difficulty in left-to-right discrimination. He may also have problems writing at the blackboard as well as copying from the board onto his paper. He has writing problems (called *dysgraphia*), which may consist of putting irregular spacing between words and letters, poor symbol making, and forming backward, jumbled, omitted, or extra letters. However, it is important for the teacher to realize that all hyperactive children will not exhibit all these symptoms because of the varying degrees of severity.

Why can't the hyperactive child learn in a group?

One reason may be that there are too many distractions and new experiences in a group, especially if it is a large one. Working in a group is difficult for the child who has an auditory perceptual problem, for when he is in a large group his brain receives a bombardment of noise and he has difficulty distinguishing important from nonimportant sounds. In a large group, it is much more difficult to maintain the structure and discipline that the child needs. Small groups of less than 12 children would be more beneficial. In a small group situation the hyperactive child is more likely to be able to advance at his own rate of development. Occasionally he should also be able to have a one-to-one relationship with his teacher.

What's the best way to handle the hyperactive child in the regular classroom?

If a child is severely hyperactive, he does not belong in a regular classroom but needs special education. As his teacher, you should bring the child's condition to the attention of the parents and proper authorities, so that he can be placed in a special classroom.

If a child is mildly hyperactive, however, several steps can be taken to make the normal classroom situation easier for both the child and the teacher. It is important to maintain a great deal of structure for him. By this I mean he should always have the same seat, within the same seating arrangement, and be placed near children who will not provoke him. It is also better to place him close to your desk so that he will pay closer attention instead of putting him in the back of the room where he can be easily distracted and neglected.

You should give him responsibilities that he can successfully carry out; this will help him feel needed and worthwhile. The tasks should be very simple at first, gradually building up to more complex ones. Your warmth and physical contact will help him and he will fare much better in a successful nonstressful situation. Therefore, if he does not answer questions properly in class, he shouldn't be embarrassed by being made fun of or by being called upon more frequently. In grading his work don't put a picture of a sad face on his papers if he hasn't done well because this will only depress him. Finally, rather than sending notes to his parents complaining about him, I recommend that you phone to discuss their child's condition with them.

What if I phone the child's parents and they refuse to recognize that their child has a problem?

It's difficult to inform parents that something is wrong with their child without hurting their feelings, and yet it is often the teacher who first recognizes that the child has a special problem. I recommend that you ask to set up a parent-teacher conference and include a third party, preferably the principal, so that the details of the conversation can be fully documented. Your approach should be simple, calm, and relaxed. First, ask the parents if they feel the child has a problem. If they answer, "No," then tell them that there is a problem in the classroom and give a typical description of what occurs at school. Then ask, "What do you think about this?" If the parents are still resistant and angry about the prospect of having a child with a deficiency, the next step would be to have the child completely tested and evaluated by the school physician, psychometrist, or school psychologist. These then would provide more of a basis for further meetings.

However, even if the physician fails to recognize the

problem and concludes that the child is "normal," this still doesn't prove that the child doesn't have a behavioral problem. As we know, many children with hyperactive behavior syndrome do have a normal physical examination, and specialized techniques must be used for a complete evaluation. The teacher should continue trying to convince the parents to seek other medical attention. Regardless of your suspicions and convictions, it is not your place as a teacher to make a diagnosis. *Diagnosis must be done by a medical specialist.*

If the parents are agreeable, more meetings should be scheduled. This will help to form a stronger liaison between the parents and the school, which will lead to a better understanding of the child. It will give the teacher a social view of the family, an awareness of the parents' expectations for their child, and an opportunity to find out about their methods of discipline. Ultimately the child will benefit by having his family and school working together in his behalf.

Learning Problems of the Hyperactive Child

What specific learning problems does the hyperactive child have?

He may have a special problem with reading because he mixes up the letters, reads them backwards, sees them upside down, or can't distinguish them from each other. For instance, he may not be able to tell a "b" from a "d," a "p" from a "q," an "h" from an "n," or a "u" from an "r." He may also have difficulty separating letters from the spaces in between words, or he may have trouble spelling. When writing or copying, he may add words, reverse numerals, skip sentences, or leave out problems. He may also have difficulty with arithmetic.

If the child has a learning problem, is he retarded?

No, not usually. The hyperactive child is usually normal or above normal in intelligence. His specific learning problem may be a visual or auditory perceptual deficit, which means that a minute part of his brain is not working correctly. Through psychological testing we can discover his range of functioning and specific abnormalities.

Why can't he read?

He may have a specific reading difficulty called *dyslexia* or he might have a *visual perceptual deficit*.

There are three different kinds of dyslexia. In *visual dyslexia*, there is a visual perception problem. In *auditory dyslexia*, the most common form, there is a problem with auditory perception. *Mixed dyslexia* is a combination of both auditory and visual dyslexia.

What is a visual perception problem?

Visual perception is the ability to acquire meaning from what one sees. Therefore, a person with a visual perception problem needs to learn to *understand* what he sees. Visual perception problems usually involve eye-motor coordination, body image and body concept, differentiating different images, and judging distance, depth, forms, position, space, patterns, and sequences.

If he has a visual perception problem, is there something physically wrong with his eyes?

No. A visual perception problem is not caused by the visual mechanism but is due to the inability of the brain to interpret correctly what the child sees. This is why hyperactive children often have reading problems and "word blindness" in school. A type of dyslexia, called *developmental dyslexia*, also occurs with non-hyperactive children of four to five years of age. They, too, commonly reverse letters, write them upside down, rotate, or distort them.

Would glasses help the child's visual perception?

No. Since visual perception takes place in the brain and not the eye, increasing the size of the visual stimuli will not increase the ability to understand what is being seen. Whether a child needs glasses depends on his *visual acuity*, which can be tested only by an examination by an optometrist or ophthalmologist.

What is an auditory perception problem?

Auditory perception is the ability to acquire meaning from sound. Therefore, if a person has an auditory perception problem he needs to learn how to *understand* what he hears. No increase in volume will increase this ability. Auditory perception problems are usually the result of a brain dysfunction. Through an auditory discrimination test such as the Wepman Test, it is possible to determine whether the child can distinguish between similar sounds, such as hush/mush, tub/tug, ta/da, pa/ba, and whether he can differentiate between sounds that are different, such as ch/sh, wa/ra, sa/za. Auditory perception problems may also affect auditory memory, which is the ability to remember time, place, and space.

Does the child with auditory perception problems have something wrong with his hearing mechanisms?

No. The hearing is ordinarily normal in the hyperactive child. However, many children suspected of mental retardation and language disorder do have hearing problems, called *auditory acuity problems*, that sometimes can be corrected with hearing aids. Generally, if a hyperactive child has an auditory problem, it is one of auditory perception only.

Why does he write his letters backwards?

This disorder may be a sign of immaturity of the central nervous system—a specific brain dysfunction. It is not caused by poor vision but by the way his brain sees the letters and reproduces them. It takes many different brain functions to see a letter, to interpret it, and then to write it correctly in its correct spatial arrangement on a piece of paper while holding the writing implement correctly. Writing the letters backwards may be a normal procedure for a 4- or 5-year-old, but it is not normal at a later time when peers are making their letters correctly.

Why is the hyperactive child better in math than in reading?

Generally the hyperactive child achieves higher scores on the math testing because this area of the brain is not as commonly affected as the higher cerebral centers that are involved with reading and writing. However, in some cases severe perceptual problems will also involve recognition, orientation, and conceptualization of numerals, figures, columns, and rows.

Why does the child have trouble pronouncing certain words?

He may have a specific deficit involving the speech zone of his brain. Pronunciation problems are also caused by muscular incoordination. Speech difficulties can also be the result of an auditory perception problem, in which the brain incorrectly perceives the sound of the words.

How can the child's learning problems be treated?

Treatment consists of a special educational prescription, which is obtained after extensive psycho-educational testing by qualified educational psychologists, and carried out by trained, experienced educational therapists. The techniques they use attempt to improve visual and auditory perception and tactile kinesthetic senses (touch and sensory stimulation). Attention is also paid to the child's coordination, balance, and posture.

The main factors in treatment are success motivation and the warm concern developed in a one-to-one relationship of teacher and child. A bond is formed between them, stimulating the child to want to please the teacher and the teacher to react positively to the child's responses and success. At first, the teacher de-emphasizes the child's problems while working on his abilities toward the goal of improving them even more. Only later are disabilities tackled.

Where can I find special education help?

A parent's first step is to discuss the child with the family physician or pediatrician, who may be able to advise them about available facilities and specialists. It is also possible to ask for treatment and assistance through the elementary school. The principal, teacher, or P.T.A. may help the parents locate an educational therapist, psychologist, or psychiatrist.

Other sources for help can be found in the telephone book listed under Special Schools, Educational Centers, Learning Centers, and Reading Centers. These may be directed by school psychologists, educational psychologists, and special teachers. Most of these are private and some are nonprofit foundations. Also, some universities and colleges have special reading centers. A word of caution: any center that advertises a positive "cure" in a short time is open to question.

What is the ideal school situation for hyperactive children?

Even though there is currently a trend toward cutting back funds for public educational facilities all over the country, we can still hope for a future when the situation will be quite different. Ideally, it should not be unreasonable to expect all children to receive the best education possible, and this should include provisions for children with special educational problems.

The way I envision it is that public schools for the educationally handicapped would be run by the local governments and would be free. They would have the best in equipment, with highly specialized teachers for the complete diagnosis, educational prescription, follow-up, and remediation of the child's problem, using a team approach for the examination and treatment of each child.

Chapter 3

Treating
the Hyperactive Child

What can we do to help our hyperactive child?

There are many ways to help your hyperactive child. The best way is to use a team approach, beginning as soon as you become aware that your child has a problem. By a team approach I mean combining special attitudes and techniques at home, seeking educational and medical diagnoses and treatment, and employing educational remediation, drug therapy, and other specialized methods where required.

Since our child has so much energy, should we let him run it off?

It is not necessary for a child to "run off" his hyperactivity; in fact, it can't be done. There is no way to get rid of all the child's energy. Of course, like all children he needs a variety of activities as outlets for his energy, so he needs to play in parks and playgrounds like other children.

Does a sports program help the hyperactive child?

Yes. A full, well-rounded education for any child includes physical activity. However, many hyperactive children move clumsily and are accident-prone, so it is especially important to select a physical education program suited to your child's abilities, one in which he will more likely be successful. It is also wise to avoid a sports program that is highly competitive, for this will only create more stress for the child.

What should we tell our other children about their hyperactive brother or sister?

First of all, be honest and don't keep your hyperactive child's condition a secret. Explain to your other children as fully as possible as much as you know about hyperactive behavior and enlist their aid. Your other children can be an invaluable help to you and their hyperactive sibling. But remember, it's as trying for them to get along with the hyperactive child as it is for you. So be sure you let them know frequently how much you appreciate their efforts and understanding. Reassure the other children that they can't "catch" their sibling's illness. Be careful not to stimulate sibling rivalry through an over-emphasis on the affected child's problems.

What should we tell our child about his own condition?

Of course, this depends on his age. You want to get across to him that you're aware he has difficulties in learning and keeping still, that you're going to get help for him, and that *he can be helped.* Above all, reassure him of your love and relieve his worries about himself by making it clear that he is not stupid, and that his capabilities are as great as those of any other child.

How can we express our feelings in such a way that he knows we love him?

Every parent should discover ways of giving love and attention freely and sincerely. Your child needs and will respond to warmth, caressing, tenderness, and concern. You can reinforce your love for him through words, smiling, and encouragement. But be careful not to overprotect him by smothering him with your love.

I am a working mother. Is there anything special I can do to help my child?

Make an extra effort to spend time alone with your child, away from interruptions. Make evenings and weekends really count in your relationship. Bedtime stories, conversations at meals, playing games, and taking trips to the zoo, museums, and other cultural events should all be carefully planned and enjoyed. Most of all, don't feel guilty because you have less time to be with your child. You needn't be apologetic about your work. Instead, make the quality of the time you have together really count. Above all, make the child feel that you really enjoy being with him.

What should I tell a babysitter about my child's condition?

It is important to explain your child's condition to your babysitter in detail, emphasizing that the child is unable to control his movements and impulses, even though he might want to. If you have certain methods of discipline, be sure to tell the babysitter what they are and give permission for her to use the same methods. This will insure that your child has some consistency in the responses that he receives. Your babysitter can be invaluable to you because she can take over while you relax and give yourself a break from the difficult task of raising a hyperactive child. However, an effective babysitter is neither an inexperienced teenager nor an aged individual but an experienced, mature, and strong person.

What can a mother do for her hyperactive boy if there is no father at home?

An uncle, grandfather, male friend, neighbor, teacher, or relative may be helpful to a mother in providing male identification for a child. However, your choice of the male image is very important. He should be a reliable man with whom your child can feel secure and at ease, and one who is understanding of the hyperactive syndrome.

How important is a daily routine to a hyperactive child?

Structure is one of the most important aids in raising a hyperactive child. He should have as much organization and structure as possible. His room should remain the same in space, color, and arrangement. His meals should be served on time. He should sit at the same place at the table. Avoid confusion and disruption as much as you can. If there is some forthcoming event or new situation, tell your child about it well in advance so that he may prepare himself. You should also be prepared for the questions that will follow and be repeated constantly.

Can we give our hyperactive child responsibilities and jobs around the house?

Yes, but it is extremely important that you give him tasks in which he is sure to succeed. Giving him responsibilities that he can handle helps raise his self-esteem through accomplishment. Also, be sure to show your appreciation for his efforts by rewarding him with kind words and sincere praise. It is important to praise him often because he isn't able to remember your praise for very long and needs constant reinforcement.

Should we let him know when we are displeased with his bad behavior, or should we just accept it?

Let him know when you are displeased. Speak frankly to him, in a firm, adult manner, and express your concern and dislike for his socially unacceptable behavior. Most important, be reasonable and consistent, and never compare his bad behavior with the good behavior of another child.

Should we punish him for bad behavior?

Yes. But, of course, avoid abusing him in any way. If you hurt him you will gradually lose his respect for your authority. There are all kinds of punishments: corporal and verbal discipline restrictions and removal of privileges. Whatever method you choose, it is important to maintain consistency. *Do as you say and carry out what you say in the same way each time.*

In disciplining your child, avoid yelling, using abusive language, striking the child, or other loss of control. Condition your child to your firm tone of voice and your facial expressions, and be consistent in what you say and do. Simple commands that are meaningful and completely understood delivered in a firm tone of voice are more successful than empty threats and statements such as, "If you're not good, I'm going to have your father punish you." The child knows that this kind of threat will not be carried out. In addition, a threat hanging over him will cause more emotional upset.

Should we spank our hyperactive child?

Sometimes parents "just feel better" after they spank their child for wrongdoing. Although I personally do not recommend spankings, if you do choose this method of punishment, make certain you only use the palm of your hand. Never hit a child with an object. If you are going to spank him, do so on his buttocks where he is the most padded. Do it immediately after he has committed his misdeed, and before spanking tell him why it is you are doing so, and afterwards ask him to tell you why he received the spanking. But remember, too frequent spankings can lose their effect.

Should the hyperactive child have a special diet?

Usually no special diet is needed, but a general, well-rounded diet with adequate and essential proteins, carbohydrates, and fats is necessary. A normal intake of vitamins, minerals, and fluids is important for maintaining good health. However, if your child's hyperactivity is caused by hypoglycemia, or if your child suffers from allergies, he may need a special diet. Dr. Ben F. Feingold, Director of the Department of Allergy at the Kaiser Permanent Medical Center in San Francisco, has reported that a restricted but nutritious diet could replace some drugs as a way to treat hyperactivity. He feels that the salicylates found in food coloring and aspirin should be avoided.

If your child has hypoglycemia, then sugar-containing foods such as fruits and bread products should be avoided, as recommended by your doctor.

Recent investigation has found that many hyperactive children are helped by drinking coffee. Caffein seems to have an effect similar to that of amphetamines—that is, it calms the child down (see Chapter 4 on drug therapy). Further research will need to be done in the area of nutrition for the hyperactive child.

I've read that some doctors are using megavitamins in treating children. Would these help my child?

Megavitamins are vitamins in large doses, many thousands of times the normal dosage. It is very rare that megavitamins will help a child with hyperactivity that is neurologically or emotionally based. On the other hand, if the child has a metabolic disturbance, megavitamins may be prescribed by the physician. These must be used with caution, especially vitamins A, D, E, and K.

There are some doctors who are now enjoying success with using megavitamins to treat autistic children (see Appendix C). It appears, however, that a two-month observation period is necessary in order to determine if there is increased social adaptation and improved psycho-educational functioning.

Would any special toys be helpful?

Buy safe, well-constructed, instructional, educational toys

that will help improve your child's perception, reading, and motor abilities. Parents can consult the child's teacher, doctor, or therapist for more specific ideas.

Can you suggest any special techniques that parents can use at home?

Yes, and sometimes these small techniques can bring big rewards. For example, because structure is very important for your child, and because he may have a problem with short-term memory, it may be advantageous to everyone to make a big chart for him. On this chart, have a checklist of those tasks that he should perform regularly, for example, "brush teeth," "wash hands and face," "dress," "comb hair," "come to the kitchen for breakfast." As he accomplishes each of these tasks, he can check them off and feel that he has done something important. This will help his self-image.

There are other methods that will help him, too. Sometimes you can have contests with him, and let him win. It is important that he receive rewards for positive behavior. Encourage any natural talents and teach him simple household skills such as breaking eggs, measuring ingredients, washing dishes, and gardening. Refrain from nagging and avoid stimulating atmospheres such as large gatherings and crowded environments.

Is there anything we can do at home for his speech problem if it is too mild for speech therapy?

Yes. A book written in 1950 by C. Van Riper, *Teaching Your Child To Talk* (Harper & Row), contains suggestions that are still useful today. The author recommends using adult conversation and discourages the use of baby talk and infantile words such as "mama" and "dada." He suggests that you not allow your child to use unacceptable words, correcting him when he mispronounces. Repeat words that you want him to understand slowly. Do not allow him to point when asking for something. Instead, insist that he respond verbally. Television shows such as "Sesame Street" and "The Electric

Company" can help with speech enrichment, as can your singing songs with him and telling each other nursery rhymes.

Can parents teach their hyperactive children themselves?

No. Special education is a highly technical field. Your child's education should be handled by the teacher and special educational therapist. However, a parent can do much to supplement school training and help the child through devices and aids for home counseling and education. This will help the child make faster progress.

What if there are no schools available for this special child?

Check with your public school principal and local board of education to see where the nearest facility for an educationally handicapped class is located. There are special laws that may apply to your child, which may enable him to receive the proper education he needs. Remember, every child should and can be educated. It is your responsibility as parents to seek the proper resources. If it is difficult to do it alone, form groups with other parents who have similar problems. There may be parent organizations already in existence that you can join, such as CANHC (see Appendix A). Through group efforts you can become better informed, call attention to your needs, contact local politicians, and eventually bring about reforms in education.

Are there any government agencies that may be helpful to a parent with children who have educational problems?

Yes. At the federal level, the Department of Health, Education, and Welfare sponsors an organization called Closer Look which provides information about the programs and agencies that are available for specific problems. Unfortunately, such organizations, which depend on federal funding, suffer from lack of money and personnel and are often unable to answer individual inquiries from parents. It may be more helpful to contact them through the public schools. In addition, individual state governments may have funds for special programs or other provisions. For example, in the state of California, most public schools have a program for the educationally handicapped that includes special day classes, learning disability group classes, and special home teachers, all funded at the state level.

Where do we go for medical treatment?

Your first step in the treatment of your child begins with your first visit to your family doctor for a medical evaluation. By discussing your child's problem with the doctor you will experience great relief in sharing your burden and by knowing that you are taking positive action to help your child. Then depending on the findings, the physician will advise you as to the next step. Do not be surprised if your child's behavior is greatly altered in front of the doctor and he finds nothing wrong. This is not unusual — those who deal with the child on a daily basis, such as teachers and parents, are usually the ones alerted first to the child's disorder. If you are not satisfied with the medical findings, or if your family doctor is unable to help you, call your local medical society and ask if they know or can recommend available developmental centers or outpatient clinics. You can also check your classified telephone directory under Clinics, especially those offering special educational and psychological services.

What kind of a doctor should we take him to?

First, seek the advice of your general physician. If he has had experience in the diagnosis, treatment, and management of the hyperactive child, he is a reliable advisor. He may wish to refer your child to a clinic, a university setting, private pediatrician, or neuropediatrician. It is also possible that he may want other referrals to the psychologist, psychiatrist, audiologist, or ophthalmologist.

Would it be better to take our child to a large medical center?

No, not necessarily. The large medical centers may be overcrowded and as yet, many do not have special clinics for the hyperactive child, nor do they have special clinics for school or learning problems. In addition, most medical centers do not have the specially trained staff or the funds to service the needs of the general population.

Is there anything special the doctor will want to know?

Yes. He will want complete detailed information on the mother's pregnancy, labor, and delivery. In addition, he will want your child's health, growth and development, and school records. Most important will be your child's behavior inventory. In Appendix D I have included some sample forms, similar to the ones your doctor may use.

It will help the physician if he can check the child's cumulative school record, the results of psychological and achievement testing, the child's grades, and teachers' comments and observations. Also, any teacher's or committee meeting reports regarding your child will provide important supplemental information.

What does the doctor usually find in his general physical examination?

Usually the physician will find the hyperactive child completely normal in the physical examination. He may also find the *hard neurological signs* to be normal as well. By hard neurological signs, we mean such tests as hitting the knee to check reflex action. However, hyperactivity is most often detected in a physical examination by checking the *soft neurological signs*, which are the more subtle indications of mild or minimal neurological impairment.

How is a diagnosis of hyperactivity made?

Unfortunately, there is no single diagnostic test. After studying the child's complete behavioral, school, and social history, the physician will do a complete physical examination which is both general and neurological. In cases where indicated he may order special neurological testing. He will next check vision and hearing and perhaps request routine laboratory work, which might include a complete blood count, urinalysis, and sugar, calcium, and glucose tolerance tests as well as tests for kidney and liver function. He may want to order a chest X ray, skull series, or bone age, but these are not always necessary. In some instances, an electroencephalogram (EEG) may be ordered to rule out the possibility of brain damage or a seizure disorder. And finally, the doctor may request certain psychological tests.

What will the laboratory tests reveal?

A complete blood count can tell the physician if the child has anemia or any other blood disorder. A glucose tolerance test can reveal low blood sugar; a urinalysis can detect sugar in the urine (an indication of possible diabetes), blood in the urine, urinary tract infections, and other kidney diseases. A bone age scan may be taken to find out if there is delayed bone development, which may indicate hypothyroidism, malnutrition and other chronic disorders such as the effects of scurvy, rickets, heavy metal intoxication, or syphilis. A thyroid study may be performed to check for high thyroid (called *hyperthyroidism*), or underactive or inactive thyroid (called *hypothyroidism*). Other laboratory investigations may include tests for calcium, blood sugar, and blood urea nitrogen (for kidney dysfunction).

On rare occasions an *amino acid chromotography* procedure may be carried out if there is a suspected metabolic disorder or mental retardation. A check on fingerprint studies (called *dermatoglyphics*) and chromosomes is not usually done unless a syndrome with physical and mental abnormalities is noted.

What will the brain tests show?

An electroencephalogram (EEG) indicates whether there is a clinical or subclinical seizure disorder or brain damage. Generally a request for this type of brain test is made if the child has a history of head injuries, any type of "spells," or abdominal pain and headaches.

Do brain tests hurt the child?

No, most certainly not. In the old days taking an electroencephalogram was painful for the patient because it required the use of needles. Fortunately today it is a painless procedure with the electrodes affixed to the scalp by means of a pastelike ointment.

What X rays are routinely called for?

X rays are not a routine procedure. However, under certain conditions they may be ordered by the physician. For example, a wrist or bone age might be taken to see if there is a correlation with the patient's chronological age and bone age. If the bone age is delayed it might correspond to a delay in growth. Or, there may be an indication of low thyroid or other disturbances. On rare occasions a skull X ray may be requested; this might indicate calcification due to an infection, an old blood clot on the brain, or a brain tumor.

What will all these tests tell the doctor about our child?

First, the tests can detect underlying abnormalities that may require treatment, such as iron deficiency anemia, low thyroid or thyroid deficiency, or psychomotor epilepsy. The tests are also useful in ruling out possible causes for your child's disorder. For example, the tests can rule out the presence of a brain tumor, chronic infections, anemia, and allergy. The results of the tests will also determine whether drug therapy is indicated and help the doctor choose the specific kind of drug for treatment. Finally, the results of psychological testing will lead to the educational prescription to be followed in managing and rehabilitating the child.

What other techniques might the doctor use for diagnosis evaluation?

There are other techniques not commonly used, such as photoelectric counters, ballistographic devices, ultrasonic devices, movies, and FM telemetric devices. But all of these are cumbersome, expensive, and too time-consuming to be routinely used in assessing hyperactivity.

Are there any simplified tests for diagnosis?

Yes. Doctors can learn to diagnose through some very basic procedures. For example, by simple observation of the child, the doctor can note whether his behavior seems to be unusual in terms of his restlessness or attention span. It is very helpful to ask the parent point blank, "Do you think your child is hyperactive?" and then to ask "Why do you think so?" This is very important, for often it is those persons who deal with the child on a daily basis who make the most astute behavioral observations.

There are also simplified screening tests that the doctor can perform in the office. The doctor may observe the child's motor movements and coordination in walking a straight line heel to toe, and while hopping, skipping, and jumping. It is also possible to test for sound-touch discrimination. To do this, the doctor makes a sound at the same moment that he touches the child to see if the child can perceive both stimuli at the same time. If the child is unable to perceive both stimuli, it may explain why he is unable to listen at times when he is busy doing other things. Another test, to determine whether the child is able to perceive two-point discrimination, is done by touching him in two different places at the same time.

Other simple methods will give the doctor further indications of possible brain dysfunction. For example, the doctor can check directionality, to discover whether the child knows his right hand from his left. The doctor can ask the child to put his right hand on his left shoulder or see if he is able to write from left to right on the paper. The doctor can also see if the child knows the top of the paper from the bottom.

Position in space can be tested to find out whether he is able to sort out different shapes from a mass of different shades of black and white. The doctor may also ask the child to draw to find out if he can hold the pencil correctly. Another test is to ask the child to make a diagonal line, a circle, a square, and a diamond. In general, a three-year-old should be able to draw a circle, a four-year-old should be able to draw a square correctly, and a five-year-old should be able to produce a diamond shape accurately. A final simple test is to ask the child how he perceives himself and his family by using the Draw-A-Person test.

Will all these tests give us a diagnosis?

Yes. After a thorough examination of the child and the test results, a medical physician can be confident in his diagnosis of the child's hyperactivity and the associated abnormalities. The physician may also make an educational diagnosis, but the educational diagnosis may also be made by a certified, qualified, and licensed psychologist. If needed, a speech pathologist can make a speech diagnosis.

Who gets the results of the diagnosis?

Upon request, and with proper authorization, a release of records in a report form can be sent to qualified people. Qualified people are physicians, social workers, teachers, principals, and psychologists. This information is confidential and is not usually sent to lay people, including the parents of the child. However, the doctor should always give a detailed explanation to the parents, and he should most certainly allow time to answer all their questions.

How will the diagnosis benefit the child?

These reports will help the child in a number of ways. First, the hyperactive child is often considered to be a "bad" child in school, and the records of his diagnosis will show the teachers and school administration that the child has a medical condition, which should make them more understanding of the child. The diagnosis will also enable the teacher to follow the educational prescription and help the school decide whether special classes are needed. In addition, the reports can help the physician by serving as a guide for drug therapy and behavior modification and management. Thus, a team effort for the control of the disorder can be started.

Is hospitalization necessary for the diagnosis?

Under ordinary conditions it is not necessary for your child to be hospitalized for diagnostic evaluation. Hospitalization is required only in the event that special tests have to be done for certain rare disorders, such as a brain tumor or metabolic disturbance. However, there are a few very specialized neuro-diagnostic facilities that may want to study the child for about a week.

I believe that an ideal diagnostic set-up would be one in which the parents would place the child in a school setting, with counselors, social workers, psychiatrists, audiologists, educational psychologists, and physicians available to test and observe the child's methods of learning, his behavioral reaction, and his response to medication. In this environment the parents could be available for continual monitoring through one-way mirrors and communication with the various specialists.

If we suspect our hyperactive child is retarded, what should we do?

After a thorough physical examination, have complete psychological testing to substantiate your impressions and to tell you the complete range of the child's functioning. Although a hyperactive child appears to be retarded and may be failing in school, tests will often indicate that his I.Q. is normal and in many instances above normal. The child's poor achievement comes about because he has specific learning disabilities, which give him a poor verbal score on standard achievement tests. At times medication may be effective in controlling the hyperactivity during the test. Test results will then be more reliable, since your child will have cooperated more with the examiner.

Does our child need to be institutionalized?

No. Institutions are for the severely mentally disturbed or the profoundly retarded, and most children can be rehabilitated at home or in smaller units such as nursing homes or foster homes.

How does a doctor treat the child who has many related problems, such as one who is hyperactive and allergic, has a seizure disorder, and who also has learning problems?

This is not an unreasonable question—I have observed many such children. After making a complete physical and neurological examination, the doctor performs an electroencephalogram and administers anticonvulsants according to the type of epilepsy indicated. While the seizure disorder is being observed, the child is given psycho-educational testing. If the child's allergies are severe and cannot be treated by withdrawing the stimuli sensitizing agent (i.e., milk, juices, berries, smoke, dust, dyes, etc.), then he should be referred to an allergist. Occasionally, antihistamines may aggravate an underlying seizure disorder, but this has not been my experience. The use of psycho-stimulants, which are behavior modifying drugs, may also be helpful in the seizure control and they are not contraindicated. In addition, the child's specific learning disability may require that he be placed in a class for the educationally handicapped or supervised by an educational therapist.

Would a psychiatrist help our child?

This depends on the severity of the hyperactivity and the associated emotional problems. A child psychiatrist is important for an initial consultation if there are indications of severe mental illness such as psychosis, autism, or schizophrenia.

What does the psychiatrist do?

The psychiatrist takes a detailed medical, psychiatric, and social history of the child, and interviews the whole family, especially the mother and father. After observing the behavior and family interactions, he then makes a diagnosis and offers suggestions. A psychiatric interview usually takes from 45 to 60 minutes and may cost from $35 to $50 per hour.

What's the difference between a psychiatrist and a psychologist?

The psychiatrist is an M.D., a physician who has taken extra training in a specialized field of psychiatry and neurology. There are also many different types of psychiatrists, each of whom prefers certain methods of treatment. A child psychiatrist would be ideal for the initial evaluation and psychotherapy.

A psychologist has a master's degree (M.A.) or doctor's degree (Ph.D.) in psychology. He specializes in psychology and has his training in psychological testing and counseling.

Would a psychologist help our child?

Yes. A psychologist is very important, especially for the administration of educational and psychological testing. In addition, the psychologist can also assist in handling parent-child relationships. If it is possible, I would advise a psychologist who specializes in child behavior.

What kind of tests will the psychologist give?

This depends upon the age and ability of the child. Generally, the psychologist will administer tests to measure intelligence, personality, and perceptual abilities. The price of each test will vary, ranging from one test at $5.00 to the Rorschach test, which costs $50. Always ask which tests are the most necessary and what are the prices of each before having them done. You should also expect to receive an explanation of the test results.

What do we do if we can't afford all the tests?

If you can't afford the testing you can wait for the public school, which eventually will probably administer some form of testing. Also, limited screening tests may be done by your private physician or pediatrician. However, if it is at all financially possible, your child should be tested.

Is there special help or psychotherapy for parents of hyperactive children, too?

Yes. Both parents should be interviewed carefully by their physician. He will be able to relieve the anxiety and guilt feelings that parents often feel. Even the strongest family can be shaken when one of its members has a behavior disturbance. If your physician deems it necessary, he may recommend individual or family counseling. There are organizations, such as CANHC in California, that print helpful reading materials, and have meetings providing guidance and moral support to parents of neurologically handicapped children. (See Appendix A.)

Would hypnosis help our child?

In certain cases hypnosis has proven to be very beneficial and as effective as intensive psychotherapy. In other cases, a combination of age regression and psychotherapy under hypnosis has been quite successful. However, it is very important that hypnosis be performed by a qualified physician.

Would a social worker be able to help us?

In circumstances of financial need a social worker who specializes in medical social work may be of value in guiding the family to the proper sources of help. The social worker is often helpful in obtaining complete details of the family history and psycho-social problems. Where necessary, the social worker may serve as a liaison between the physician, family, and school.

Would a speech therapist be of any help?

If the child has specific speech deficits, the speech therapist can help him with pronunciation, articulation, voice control, rhythm, and breathing.

What should we do if we can't afford professional help?

It is important to "put all your irons in the fire." First check with the P.T.A. at your local school to see if they know of a special neurology clinic. Call the clinics at university teaching hospitals and other private hospitals and guidance centers in your area. Call on your United Way agency and check their Directory of Information and Referral Services to see if there are any special facilities for which you would qualify for assistance.

Chapter 4

Drug Therapy
and Hyperactivity

Does my hyperactive child need drugs?

Probably. Many children require medication to control their hyperactive behavior or to allow them to handle the emotional difficulties that have been learned, conditioned, and reinforced. This medication may be helpful in the *initial* phases of therapy. Therapists often will not take a hyperactive child unless he is taking some medication that will enable him to cooperate. Medication may be the only thing that allows the child to remain in school in a calm, relaxed way so that he can learn. The medication helps the child break the emotional and behavioral cycle of hyperactivity, calming him down so that he is able to learn new and productive responses and to relate to his environment in a positive way. Yet medication alone is not the answer. It is of utmost importance that drug therapy be combined with educational therapy and counseling where indicated. Maximum effectiveness will be gained only through this combination of treatments.

However, not every hyperactive child needs drug therapy. Although 75 percent of the children who have organically based hyperactivity respond well to medication, unnecessary medication for the purpose of restraint and control of emotionally maladjusted children cannot be condoned. The rule should be that *if a desired effect can be obtained without medication then it should not be used.* Some children will respond equally well to other forms of therapy, such as parent counseling, psychotherapy, and educational therapy.

How long should drug therapy be used?

It depends upon the child's problem and how effective the therapy is. Medication may be withdrawn after three to six months to see if the behavioral and emotional cycles have been broken and if the child can do well without it. On the other hand, many hyperactive children have to be on medication for years, sometimes up to adolescence. The decision to terminate drugs is left to the physician.

What are the different kinds of medications that are used?

What medication the doctor prescribes depends on the cause and type of the child's hyperactivity. Generally these medications fall into four major categories: sedatives, stimulants, tranquilizers, and anticonvulsants.

What are sedatives, and when are they used?

The most common sedatives are barbiturates such as phenobarbital, Mebarol®, or methbarbital. Sedatives were first used in the treatment of hyperactivity in the 1930s. These drugs are intended to have a calming effect upon the child; however, they often produce the opposite of the desired effect, stimulating the child's insomnia, increasing the hyperactivity and irritability, and causing headaches. In some cases barbiturates can also be used effectively as anticonvulsants.

What are stimulants and when are they used?

Stimulants are used very successfully in the treatment of organic hyperactivity. One important class of these medications are the amphetamines, such as Dexedrine®, Benzedrine®, Deaner®, and Dexamyl®. Amphetamines usually speed up the metabolism and make the patient more alert and active. They are known as "uppers" or "bennies." However, when used in the treatment of hyperactivity they produce a reverse effect and actually calm the child down. These drugs bring about amazing results within ten minutes after ingestion, making the child calm, attentive, and cooperative, and improving his learning and perceptual abilities. Generally, the use of amphetamines will not only make the child less distractible, they will also raise testing and I.Q. scores.

Certain side effects may occur from amphetamine intake such as loss of appetite, poor sleep habits, and weight loss, but these may be minimized through the use of vitamins and food supplements and withdrawal of medication on weekends or every three or four days. Another negative effect of amphetamines is that, since there is a great tolerance to these drugs, the dosage must sometimes have to be increased in order to be effective.

Another kind of stimulant that is used in Ritalin® (methylphenidate). It is a mild anti-depressant and one that is very useful in the treatment of hyperactivity. It has all the attributes of the amphetamines but produces less loss of appetite, less weight loss, and less depression and irritability when it wears off. However, Ritalin® may produce nervousness and insomnia or in some cases have the same side effects as the amphetamines. Sometimes negative effects can be controlled by reducing the dosage or omitting the drug in the afternoon and evening. Remember that your child's reaction is individual.

How are stimulants given?

Amphetamines are usually administered after the child has

eaten in order to avoid appetite loss, while Ritalin® is ordinarily given before meals. I like to start with a small quantity, such as ½ tablet before breakfast for five days, increasing to ½ tablet before breakfast and before lunch. This dosage can be increased until the desired behavior is attained. I start off with small doses and increase the dosage gradually in order to minimize the possible side effects.

Are stimulants habit forming?

No, not usually in children. However, teenagers and adults may become addicted to high dosages and become drug abusers. The way to avoid this is to stop the use of stimulants before the child reaches adolescence.

What if the medication makes him depressed and too quiet?

Ritalin® sometimes does have this negative effect. If this occurs, I usually stop the medication completely for three or four days. Then I start out giving one half the usual dosage. If no side effects or negative effects are noticed, then I increase the dosage gradually. Remember, the effectiveness of certain drugs depends upon body weight and particular reactions of the individual.

What are tranquilizers and when are they used?

Tranquilizers, called *psychotropic agents*, have a calming effect on hyperactive children, particularly when the cause of the hyperactivity is emotional rather than organic. Tranquilizers are known by various names, such as Thorazine®, Mellaril®, Atarax®, Stelazine®, and other phenolthiozines. However, because the cause of the hyperactivity is emotional, medication without appropriate psychotherapy will only do half the job. It takes a few weeks before an evaluation of the effects of tranquilizers can be made. Occasional side effects may include lowered blood pressure and retinal pigmentation.

What are anticonvulsants and when are they used?

Dilantin® is a commonly used anticonvulsant, and its use must be carefully monitored. It is generally used only for children with clinical seizures or psychomotor epilepsy. Generally, it is given in small dosages, and often Ritalin® is prescribed to make its effect more powerful. Dilantin® comes in chewable tablets, liquid, and capsule form. In some cases it may cause a puffy gum condition called *hyperplasia*, which is not serious and which will disappear when the medication is discontinued if the child receives proper dental care.

As mentioned earlier, the sedatives phenobarbital and Mebarol® are also used as anticonvulsants for major motor seizures or psychomotor epilepsy. However, when phenobarbital is being used the child's test results may be negatively affected and there may be a decrease in attention and learning, as well as sleepiness caused by too strong a dosage. It is therefore important to monitor all drugs carefully.

Are there any other side effects caused by anticonvulsants?

Not usually. Very rarely, kidney trouble or blood disease may develop from these medications, so it is very important that a blood count and urinalysis be done every three or four months. This is especially true for Dilantin® and similar drugs.

Are anticonvulsant drugs habit forming?

No. Most of these drugs do not seem to be habit forming. However, they should be withdrawn gradually after the seizures have been controlled for two to five years.

What other kinds of medications can be used to treat hyperactivity?

In 25 percent of hyperactive children Benadryl®, an antihistamine used for allergy and itching, has a calming effect. Its beneficial effect is in giving these children mild sedation, but this usually also causes their reactions in testing to be delayed or slower than normal.

Are there any new drugs coming out that look promising?

Several drug companies are experimenting to develop the ideal drug, one that would have a calming effect, increase the attention span, increase the ability to learn and remember, and not have side effects or become habit forming. They are looking for a medication that would not produce the side effects of weight loss, poor appetite, personality change, and sleeplessness, or diminish any other brain function. Ideally, this drug would be inexpensive and easily tolerated.

Is it necessary to give medication at the same time every day?

Most medications should be given at a consistent time so as not to confuse the child. A regular medication routine will help reassure him. However, each drug differs. For example, anticonvulsants can be given at any time during the day, up to four times a day. The important thing here is to maintain a particular blood level so that the brain remains calm.

Ritalin® should ordinarily be given before or at breakfast. Amphetamines are usually administered after breakfast so at least one good meal will be eaten before the appetite is affected. Also the effect of amphetamines may wear off in from four to eight hours. Therefore it is important to give it at an early time so that your child will remain calm during school and be able to learn.

If our child is more unmanageable on some days, should we increase the dosage of his medicine?

This may become necessary, and a half tablet or an extra tablet at certain stressful times may be the solution to the problem. Then again, when your child does not need the medication—for example, on weekends when he is free from the stress and frustration of school—medication should be discontinued or gradually reduced. However, *do not make any change in his dosage without first consulting your doctor.*

Should we take our child off drugs during holidays?

It depends. Many children do not need medication during holidays and for these children it should be discontinued. However, it is important to have the medication available, especially during a vacation when the other members of the family want to enjoy themselves completely. Remember, medication does not make the child dependent. What it does is help him form a new habit of psychological adaptation, giving him the ability to overcome frustration so that this learned behavior can be carried on without the medication.

What do we do if the medication ruins his appetite?

There are two alternatives. You can change the medication to one that does not affect the appetite, or you can increase the child's caloric intake. Do this by giving him nutritional snacks such as milkshakes during the afternoon or before he goes to bed. Adding B-complex vitamins and Periactin® may also increase his appetite.

Will the child revert to his ordinary state after the pill has worn off?

It depends on the stress he experiences. For example, he will generally be better without medication during the summer vacation than during the school year. Most hyperactive children will improve with age and the reconditioning of behavior that the medication allows.

Will he need medication for the rest of his life?

Probably not. There are very few hyperactive adults who require medication. In general, medication is most effective before adolescence. During adolescence I do not recommend it unless absolutely required for the treatment of an underlying seizure disorder, in which case anticonvulsants should be continued.

Will medication make our child emotionally handicapped?

No. If the diagnosis of the child was correct, the right medication will facilitate his development, increase his ability to pay attention, and allow him to make judgments in directing his own behavior. Medication enables the child to break a negative behavior cycle, replacing it with one that is positive and that brings him rewards. The use of medication therefore does not handicap the child. On the contrary, it helps set the stage for satisfactory psychological and emotional development.

Does drug therapy ever produce serious side effects?

Long-term use of *any* medication may produce problems. That is why drugs must be carefully monitored by the physician and be administered in proper dosages. Excessive medication can cause weight loss, insomnia, poor school achievement, mental deterioration, or deterioration in perception and coordination. Any one of these symptoms is an indication that withdrawal and discontinuance of the drug may be needed. Any change in your child's reaction should be reported to your doctor immediately.

Is there a risk of drug dependency in later life?

Thirty years of clinical experience and several scientific studies have failed to establish association between the medical use of stimulants in the preadolescent child and later drug abuse. Physicians who care for children treated with stimulants have noted that the children do not experience pleasurable subjective effects that would encourage misuse, observing that most often the child is willing to stop the drug therapy, which he views as "medicine."

Similarly in the treatment of epilepsy, barbiturates have been given from infancy to adulthood without creating problems of dependency or abuse. It is important to note that it is ordinarily not the drug itself that causes abuse but the way in which the drug and its effects are used and exploited by an individual. There are indeed nonhyperactive adolescents who either misuse or dangerously abuse stimulants by experimenting with the effects of excessive dosage to create excitement, to avoid sleep, to defy constraints and authority in parents, and to combat fatigue and gloom. But it should be noted that these drugs are not commonly prescribed to hyperactive children after the age of 11 or 12, when the risk of such experimentation or misuse might possibly become more significant.

Are there any safeguards against drug misuse?

The best safeguard is to use all drugs under strict medical supervision. In addition, there are some sensible steps parents can take to guard against possible misuse. The child should never be given sole responsibility for taking the medication. If he has to take the medication during school hours, it can be dispensed by the school nurse at a given time. The precautions that prevail regarding any medicines, whether they be antibiotics, aspirins, sedatives, or other medications, should be applied not only to the affected child, but to all children in the family. Remember, any medicine can be misused, and if taken incorrectly any drug can be dangerous.

Chapter 5

Your Child's Future

What will happen to our hyperactive child if he goes untreated?

His exact future cannot be predicted with certainty. Some hyperactive children can grow up to appear completely normal, while others become hyperactive adults. However, even those who "outgrow" the disorder are likely to exhibit some emotional difficulties as the result of their childhood disorder if the disorder is not treated.

Some studies indicate that severe and long-range emotional disturbances may result in a certain number of adults being confined to mental institutions. Other studies show that the untreated hyperactive child has a higher tendency for school failure and juvenile delinquency. One study of juvenile delinquents found that many had specific learning problems and that hyperactivity was a common symptom of their past. The results were not surprising, since we know that emotional disturbances become aggravated as learning problems develop and frustration levels increase.

The untreated hyperactive child has less chance of succeeding in the future. His job future is an immense problem if he is not treated at an early age. He may have a history of repeated school failure. His emotional problems may make him afraid of school, causing him to run away or drop out. If he is given no opportunity for rehabilitation, he will end up being a nonreader, falsely believing that he is stupid and unable to read. Out of frustration, he may turn to crime as an answer.

I cannot emphasize enough the importance of early recognition and treatment of specific educational disabilities for the benefit of the hyperactive child's emotional, physical, and economic future.

Will my child ever be able to go to college?

This, of course, depends on the level of his intelligence, the degree of associated defects, and early initiation of treatment. Most children will outgrow their hyperactivity and will be able to go to college and have very successful careers.

Others can seek jobs that do not require any reading, writing, or spelling skills. They may work in the manual trades, such as plumbing or mechanics. Eventually a few find themselves able to do certain mechanical skills expertly; however, the majority of hyperactive children have poor coordination and have difficulty developing mechanical proficiency.

Is it more realistic to plan on his going to a technical school?

Again, it depends on the individual child, his abilities, and of course, his desires. Technical school is designed for those with higher mechanical than verbal abilities and if your child has these abilities they should be encouraged.

What kind of person will he grow up to be?

Through effective and early treatment, the hyperactive child can grow up to be a productive person who has overcome his handicap. With your love and acceptance of him as an individual, he can learn to be economically self-sufficient and emotionally well adjusted. He can become a person who is able to give and receive love—the goal of every human being.

Appendix A

Where to Get Help

Alabama

Alabama Foundation to Aid Aphasoid Children
P.O. Box 6103
Birmingham, Alabama 35209

Association for Children with Learning Disabilities
Mrs. Edna Thompson
912 S. 81st Street
Birmingham, Alabama 35206

Auburn University
School of Education
Reading Clinic
Auburn, Alabama

Huntsville Achievement School
212 Eustis Street (Box 835)
Huntsville, Alabama 35804

Shades Cahaba Elementary School
Aphasoid School
3001 Montgomery Highway
Homewood, Alabama 36830

Smaban Psychiatric Clinic
Medical College
Reading Disability Center and Clinic
Birmingham, Alabama

University of Alabama
College of Education
Reading Laboratory
University, Alabama 35486

University of Alabama Medical Center
Department of Pediatrics
Clinic for Developmental and Learning Disorders
1919 7th Avenue South
Birmingham, Alabama

Arizona

Arizona State University
College of Education
Dept. of Elementary Education
Reading Center
Tempe, Arizona 85281

Cerebral Palsy Foundation of Southern Arizona Inc.
3825 East Second Street
Tucson, Arizona

Children's Evaluation Center of Southern Arizona
1 South Quadrante Street
Tucson, Arizona

Northern Arizona University
Department of Special Education
Flagstaff, Arizona

University of Arizona
College of Education
Reading Service Center
Tucson, Arizona 85721

University of Arizona
Dept. of Psychology
Psychological Clinic
Tucson, Arizona

Arizona Assoc. for Children with Learning Disabilities
P.O. Box 15525
Phoenix, Arizona 85018

Arizona Assoc. for Children with Learning Disabilities
Jeanne LaBouff
P.O. Box 11384
Phoenix, Arizona 85017

Arkansas

University of Arkansas
Dept. of Psychiatry
Division of Child Psychiatry
Medical Center
Little Rock, Arkansas

Arkansas Assoc. for Children with Learning Disabilities
Mrs. Richard Newby
Drawer A
Pulaski Heights Station
Little Rock, Arkansas 72205

California

California Assoc. for Neurologically Handicapped Children
P.O. Box 45273
Los Angeles, California

Dubnoff School for Education Therapy
10526 Victory Place
North Hollywood, California 91606

Escalon, Inc.
536 E. Mendocino Street
Altadena, California 91001

Frostig Center for Educational Therapy
5981 Venice Blvd.
Los Angeles, California 90034

Gateways Community Mental Health Center
Hyperkinetic Children's Clinic
1891 Effie Street
Los Angeles, California 90026

Glassell Park Growth & Development Center
3303 Division Street
Los Angeles, California 90065

Harmony Center
26204 Veva Way
Calabasas, California 91032

Kennedy Child Study Center, Inc.
1339 20th Street
Santa Monica, California 90404

California Assoc. for Neurologically Handicapped Children
John Robertson
5709 North Pleasant
Fresno, California 93705

Canada

Canadian Assoc. for Children with Learning Disabilities
88 Eglington Avenue East
Suite 322
Toronto, 315, Ontario

Colorado

Children's Hospital
Dept. of Audiology and Speech Pathology
1056 E. 19th Street
Denver, Colorado

Colorado State University
Dept. of Hearing and Speech Science
Speech and Hearing Clinic
Fort Collins, Colorado

Randell School of Denver
2160 S. Cook Street
Denver, Colorado

The Reading Clinic
1246 Toedtli
Boulder, Colorado

University of Colorado
Speech & Hearing Clinic
934 Broadway
Boulder, Colorado

University of Denver
Dept. of Speech Pathology and Audiology

Speech & Hearing Center
University Park Campus
Denver, Colorado 80210

Western State College
Dept. of Education
Gunnison, Colorado 81230

Colorado Assoc. for Children with Learning Disabilities
Lawrence E. Brady
828 Seventeenth Street
Denver, Colorado 80202

Colorado Assoc. for Children with Learning Disabilities
% George D. Moller, President
P.O. Box #1506
Denver, Colorado 80201

Connecticut

Foster School Inc.
315 South Ronan Street
New Haven, Connecticut 06511

The Foundation School, Inc.
P.O. Box 719
Orange, Connecticut 06477

Grove School
Madison, Connecticut

The Ives School for Special Children
185 Cold Spring Street
New Haven, Connecticut 06517

Persons Reading School, Inc.
10 Arch Street
Norwalk, Connecticut 06850

Whitby School
969 Lake Avenue
Greenwich, Connecticut 06830

Connecticut Assoc. for Children with Perceptual Learning
    Disabilities
Mrs. Beatrice E. Benton
14 Rockwell Place
West Hartford, Connecticut 06107

Connecticut Assoc. for Children with Learning Disabilities
Mrs. Ruth Tepper, President
20 Raymond Road
West Hartford, Connecticut 06107

Delaware

University of Delaware
Department of Education
Reading Study Center
Newark, Delaware

Diamond State Assoc. for Children with Learning Disabilities
S. Lup Jung
1508 Emory Road
Wilmington, Delaware 19803

Diamond State Assoc. for Children with Learning Disabilities
Mr. Thomas C. McGowan
P.O. Box 177
Claymont, Delaware 19703

District of Columbia

The American University Clinic for Learning Disabilities
Department of Education
Washington, D.C. 20016

George Washington University
Psychological Clinic
718 21st Street, N.W.
Washington, D.C. 20006

The Kingsbury Center for Remedial Education
2138 Bancroft Place, N.W.
Washington, D.C. 20008

Washington D.C. Assoc. for Children with Learning Disabilities
Robert Jackson
627 Allison Street, N.W.
Washington, D.C. 20011

Closer Look
Box 1492
Washington, D.C. 20013

Florida

Deerborne School
311 Sevilla Avenue
Coral Gables, Florida

Diagnostic & Evaluation Clinic
2350 Lakeview Avenue South
St. Petersburg, Florida 33712

Green Valley School at the Monastery
Orange City, Florida 32763

Learning Disability School
Exceptional Child Center
425 S.W. 28th Street
Fort Lauderdale, Florida

The Mills School
1512 East Broward Blvd.
Fort Lauderdale, Florida

Reading Education & Development Clinic
330 West Platt Street
Tampa, Florida 33606

University of Florida
College of Education
Personnel Services Dept.
Children's Learning Center
Gainesville, Florida

University of Florida
Dept. of Comprehensive English
Reading Laboratory & Clinic
310 Anderson Hall
Gainesville, Florida

University of Miami
Dept. of Special Education
Child Development Center
Coral Gables, Florida 33124

University of Miami
Guidance Center
Reading Clinic
Coral Gables, Florida 33124

The Vanguard School
P.O. Box 928
Lake Wales, Florida

Florida Assoc. for Children with Learning Disabilities
℅ Lars Dohm, President
P.O. Box #3861
St. Petersburg, Florida 33731

Georgia

Emory University
Division of Teacher Education
Atlanta Speech School
2020 Peachtree Road, N.W.
Atlanta, Georgia 30309

Georgia Assoc. for Children with Learning Disabilities
Dr. R. Wayne Jones
P.O. Box 27507
Atlanta, Georgia 30327

Georgia Assoc. for Children with Learning Disabilities
Mrs. Betty H. Lockett
P.O. Box #29492
Atlanta, Georgia 30329

Hawaii

The Reading Clinic
1611 Keeaumoku Street
Room 209
Honolulu, Hawaii

Variety Club School
1212 University Ave.
Honolulu, Hawaii 96814

Waialae Catholic Center
4449 Malia Street
Honolulu, Hawaii

Hawaii Assoc. for Children with Learning Disabilities
Mrs. ViDolman
P.O. Box 10187
Honolulu, Hawaii 96816

Hawaii Assoc. for Children with Learning Disabilities
Max Templeman
P.O. Box #4203
Honolulu, Hawaii 96813

Idaho

Idaho State University
Dept. of Speech Pathology & Audiology
Speech & Hearing Center
Box 116
Pocatello, Idaho

Idaho Assoc. for Children with Learning Disabilities
Mrs. Dianne Hickey
808 17th Avenue South
Nampa, Idaho 83651

Illinois

Bradley University
School of Speech Therapy
Peoria, Illinois 61606

Cook County Hospital
Dept. of Pediatrics
1825 W. Harrison St.
Chicago, Illinois 60612

The Day School
800 Buena Avenue
Chicago, Illinois 60613

Illinois College of Optometry
Clinic Dept.
3241 South Michigan Avenue
Chicago, Illinois

Keith Country Day School
1715 North 2nd Street
Rockford, Illinois 61108

Little Company of Mary Hospital
Dept. of Speech & Hearing Services
2800 W. 95th Street
Evergreen Park, Illinois

Loyola University Guidance Center
820 N. Michigan Avenue
Chicago, Illinois

Michael Reese Hospital
Henner Hearing & Speech Center
Dept. of Hearing & Speech-Otolaryngology
2929 S. Ellis Avenue
Chicago, Illinois

National College of Education
Guidance Center
2840 Sheridan Road
Evanston, Illinois 60201

Northwestern University
Dept. of Communicative Disorders
1831 Harrison
Evanston, Illinois

Presbyterian-St. Luke's Hospital
Dept. of Pediatrics
1753 W. Congress Parkway
Chicago, Illinois

Ravinia Reading & Educational Clinic, Inc.
580 Roger Williams Avenue
Highland Park, Illinois

Rockford College
Dept. of Education Evening College
Reading Clinic
5050 East State Street
Rockford, Illinois 61101

Schwab Hospital
Dept. of Psychology, Speech, and Audiology
1401 S. California
Chicago, Illinois

University of Chicago
Dept. of Education
Speech & Language Clinic
950 E. 59th Street
Chicago, Illinois 60637

University of Illinois
Medical Center
Center for Handicapped Children
840 S. Wood Street
Chicago, Illinois 60612

Illinois Council for Children with Learning Disabilities
Mrs. Bert P. Schloss
P.O. Box 656
Evanston, Illinois 60204

Illinois Assoc. for Children with Learning Disabilities
Mr. Robert Kelly
Post Office Box #9239
Chicago, Illinois 60690

Indiana

The Guidance Center of St. Mary's College
State Theatre Building
214 South Michigan Street
South Bend, Indiana 46601

Indiana State University
Dept. of Special Education
Speech & Hearing Clinic
Terre Haute, Indiana 47809

Indiana University Medical Center
Dept. of Pediatric Neurology
1100 W. Michigan
Indianapolis, Indiana

Indiana Assoc. for Perceptually Handicapped Children
Robert H. Yarman
Route 2
Cable Trail
Fort Wayne, Indiana 46805

Indiana Assoc. for Children with Learning Disabilities
Mr. LeLand Montgomery
1507 South Parker Drive
Evansville, Indiana 47714

Iowa

Iowa College of Education
Children's Reading Clinic
Iowa City, Iowa 52240

State College of Iowa
Educational Clinic
Speech Clinic
Cedar Falls, Iowa 50613

University Hospital School
Department of Pediatrics
Child Development Clinic
Iowa City, Iowa

Iowa Assoc. for Children with Learning Disabilities
Val L. Schoenthal
5105 Waterbury Road
Des Moines, Iowa 50312

Iowa Assoc. for Children with Learning Disabilities
% Mr. L. C. Bader
6107 Woodland Road
Des Moines, Iowa 50312

Kansas

Fort Hays Kansas State College
Division of Education & Psychology
Psychological Service Center
Hays, Kansas 67601

Institute of Logopedics
2400 Jardine Drive
Wichita, Kansas 67219

Kansas State Teachers College
Department of Counseling Services
Emporia, Kansas

University of Kansas
Dept. of Psychology
Psychological Clinics
307 Fraser Hall
Lawrence, Kansas 66044

University of Kansas Medical Center
Children's Rehabilitation Unit
Rainbow at 39th Street
Kansas City, Kansas

Kansas Assoc. for Children with Learning Disabilities
% Harriet H. Harris
24 Willowbrook
Wichita, Kansas 67207

Kentucky

Louisville General Hospital
Dept. of Pediatrics
Child Evaluation Center
323 E. Chestnut Street
Louisville, Kentucky 40202

Morehead State University
Dept. of Psychology
Morehead, Kentucky

Norton Psychiatric Clinic
Dept. of Psychiatry
231 W. Oak Street
Louisville, Kentucky

Kentucky Assoc. for Children with Learning Disabilities Inc.
James T. Eisman
P. O. Box 7171
Louisville, Kentucky 40207

Louisiana

Cerebral Palsy Center of Greater Baton Rouge
1805 College Drive
Baton Rouge, Louisiana 70808

Grambling College
Special Education Center
Grambling, Louisiana

The Hew School
P. O. Box 26093
4018 Downman Road
New Orleans, Louisiana

Louisiana Polytechnic Institute
Dept. of Special Education
P. O. Box 1857
Tech Station
Ruston, Louisiana

Louisiana State University
Dept. of Education
Special Education Center
Room 45 Field House
Baton Rouge, Louisiana 70803

Louisiana State University
Dept. of Speech
Speech & Hearing Clinic
Baton Rouge, Louisiana 70803

Louisiana State University in New Orleans
Special Education Center
Lakefront
New Orleans, Louisiana

The Magnolia School, Inc.
100 Central Avenue
New Orleans, Louisiana 70122

Northeast Louisiana State College
Dept. of Special Education
Special Education Center
Monroe, Louisiana

Northwestern State College
Dept. of Special Education
Special Education Center
Natchitoches, Louisiana

University of Southwestern Louisiana
Dept. of Special Education
Special Education Center
Box 515 N.S.L.
Lafayette, Louisiana

Louisiana Assoc. for Children with Learning Disabilities
James Rigsby
719 Texas
Shreveport, Louisiana 71101

Louisiana Assoc. for Children with Learning Disabilities
2950 Hearne Avenue
Shreveport, Louisiana 71103

Maine

Winter Harbor Reading School
Winter Harbor, Maine 04693

Maryland

Coppin State College
Dept. of Special Education
2500 W. North Avenue
Baltimore, Maryland

Easter Seal Treatment Center of the Montgomery County Society
for Crippled Children & Adults, Inc.
1000 Twinbrook Parkway
Rockville, Maryland 20851

Johns Hopkins Hospital
Division of Audiology & Speech
Hearing & Speech Center
Baltimore, Maryland 21205

Homewood School Reading Clinic
4906 Roland Avenue
Baltimore, Maryland 21210

University of Maryland Hospital
Dept. of Pediatrics
Clinic for the Exceptional Child
Redwood & Greene Streets
Baltimore, Maryland

University of Maryland
Dept. of Education
Reading Center
College Park, Maryland

Maryland Assoc. for Children with Learning Disabilities
Jay B. Cutler
320 Maryland National Bank Building
Baltimore, Maryland 21202

Maryland Assoc. for Children with Learning Disabilities
Mrs. Joan Rupp, President
18805 Muncastor Road
Derwood, Maryland 20855

Massachusetts

Boston School for the Deaf
Aphasic Department
800 N. Main Street
Randolph, Massachusetts

Boston University
School of Education
Educational Clinic
765 Commonwealth Avenue
Boston, Massachusetts

Boston University
Dept. of Special Education
Psycho-Educational Clinic
765 Commonwealth Avenue
Boston, Massachusetts 02115

Children's Hospital Medical Center
The Adolescents Unit
300 Longwood Avenue
Boston, Massachusetts 02115

Eagle Hill School
Mardwick, Massachusetts

The Kingsley School
397 Marlborough Street
Boston, Massachusetts

Massachusetts General Hospital
Language Clinic
Fruit Street
Boston, Massachusetts

New England Medical Center Hospitals
Speech, Hearing & Language Center
171-185 Harrison Avenue
Boston, Massachusetts 02111

Perceptual Education & Research Center
57 Grove Street
Wellesley, Massachusetts 02181

The Reading Institute of Boston
116 Newbury Street
Boston, Massachusetts 02116

Reading Research Institute
32 Locust Avenue
Lexington, Massachusetts

State College
Dept. of Special Education
Fitchburg, Massachusetts

University of Massachusetts
Dept. of Education
Amherst, Massachusetts 01002

Worcester Youth Guidance Center
Dept. of Psychology
Belmont Street
Worcester, Massachusetts

Massachusetts Child Assoc. for Children with Learning
    Disabilities
Dr. Raymond E. Sparks
30 Worthen Street B10
Chelmsford, Massachusetts 01824

Massachusetts Assoc. for Children with Learning Disabilities
Nancy Brown
207 Pleasant Street
Marlboro, Massachusetts 01752

Massachusetts Child Assoc. for Children with Learning
    Disabilities Inc.
% Paul Morris, President
949 Commonwealth Avenue
Boston, Massachusetts 02215

Michigan

Calvin Psychological Institute
Psychological Dept.
752 Giddings, S.E.
Grand Rapids, Michigan

Central Michigan University
Dept. of Education
Psycho-Educational Clinic
Mt. Pleasant, Michigan 48858

Central Michigan University
Dept. of Speech & Drama
Speech & Hearing Clinic
Mt. Pleasant, Michigan

Children's Orthogenic School
10235 W. 7 Mile Road
Detroit, Michigan 48221

Marygrove College
Speech & Hearing Clinic
8425 W. McNichols
Detroit, Michigan 48221

University of Michigan
Division of Reading Improvement Services
Bureau of Psychological Services
1610 Washtenaw
Ann Arbor, Michigan

Wayne State University
Dept. of Educational Psychology
Learning Abilities Laboratory
341 Education Building
Detroit, Michigan

Wayne State University
Dept. of Speech & Special Education
Speech & Hearing Center
5900 Second Avenue
Detroit, Michigan 48202

Michigan Assoc. for Children with Learning Disabilities
Mrs. W.E. Hinrichsen
P. O. Box 743
Royal Oak, Michigan 48068

Michigan Assoc. for Children with Learning Disabilities
Mr. Albert Katzman, President
2961 Orchard Place
Orchard Lake, Michigan 48033

Minnesota

Gillette State Hospital for Crippled Children
Dept. of Schooling
1003 East Ivy Avenue
St. Paul, Minnesota 55106

St. Cloud State College
Dept. of Special Education
St. Cloud, Minnesota 56301

University of Minnesota
Dept. of Speech
Duluth, Minnesota

Minnesota Assoc. for Children with Learning Disabilities
Mrs. Keith Slettehaugh
1900 Chicago Avenue
Minneapolis, Minnesota 55404

Minnesota Assoc. for Children with Learning Disabilities
Mr. Gene Quist, President
1821 University
St. Paul, Minnesota 55104

Mississippi

University of Mississippi
University Medical Center
Dept. of Pediatrics
Child Development Clinic
Jackson, Mississippi

University of Southern Mississippi
Dept. of Speech & Hearing Sciences
Special Education & Psychological Clinic
Southern Station
Hattiesburg, Mississippi

Mississippi Assoc. for Children with Learning Disabilities
Fred C. Bradley
P. O. Box 12083
Jackson, Mississippi 39211

Missouri

Central Institute for Deaf
Dept. of Outpatient Clinics & School
818 S. Euclid
St. Louis, Missouri

Menorah Medical Center
Hearing & Speech Center
4949 Rockhill Road
Kansas City, Missouri

Miriam School
524 Bismarck Ave.
Webster Groves, Missouri 63119

Missouri State Teachers College
Dept. of Special Programs
Reading Clinic
Speech & Hearing Clinic
Violette Hall
Kirksville, Missouri 63501

Psychological Associates
8220 Delmar
St. Louis, Missouri 63124

St. Louis University
Dept. of Speech
Speech & Hearing Clinics
15 N. Grand Blvd.
St. Louis, Missouri

University of Missouri Medical Center
Multiple Handicap Clinic
Building TD-4
Columbia, Missouri

Missouri Assoc. for Children with Learning Disabilities
Mrs. W. Yates Trotter, Jr.
P. O. Box 3303
Glenstone Station
Springfield, Missouri 65804

Montana

Eastern Montana College
Center for Handicapped Children & Reading Clinic
1500 N. 30th Street
Billings, Montana

Montana Assoc. for Children with Learning Disabilities
Mrs. Violet Kueffler
Box 2563
Great Falls, Montana 59401

Montana Assoc. for Children with Learning Disabilities
% Mrs. Don Espelin, President
P. O. Box #751
Helena, Montana 59601

Nebraska

Creighton Memorial St. Joseph's Hospital
Dept. of Speech & Hearing
2305 S. 10th Street
Omaha, Nebraska

Union College
Dept. of Education & Psychology
3800 S. 48th Street
Lincoln, Nebraska

University of Nebraska
College of Medicine
Department of Pediatrics
Evaluation & Counseling Clinic
Omaha, Nebraska

University of Nebraska
Dept. of Speech & Dramatic Art
Speech & Hearing Laboratory
12th and R Streets
Lincoln, Nebraska

Nebraska Assoc. for Children with Learning Disabilities
Mr. & Mrs. Allen Dudley
P. O. Box #6464
Omaha, Nebraska 68106

Nevada

College of Education
Teaching & Resource Center
Reading Clinic
10 Artemisia Way
Reno, Nevada 89507

New Hampshire

Dartmouth Medical School
Child Psychiatry Division
Hanover, New Hampshire

New Hampshire Assoc. for Children with Learning Disabilities
E.M. Still
118 Donahue Drive
Manchester, New Hampshire 03103

New Hampshire Assoc. for Children with Learning Disabilities
Mrs. Ann Campbell
20 Westbourne Road
Concord, New Hampshire 03301

New Jersey

Center for Child & Adolescent Development
16 Grove Avenue
Verona, New Jersey

Glassboro State College
Dept. of Education
Diagnostic & Consultation Center
Glassboro, New Jersey 08028

Lord Stirling Schools Inc.
Lord Stirling Road
Basking Ridge, New Jersey

Newark State College
Dept. of Special Education
Child Study Center
Union, New Jersey 07083

State College
Dept. of Education
Reading Clinic
Union, New Jersey

Trenton State College
Child Study & Demonstration Center
Trenton, New Jersey

New Jersey Assoc. for Children with Learning Disabilities
Mr. Robert Winnerman, President
P. O. Box #249
Convent Station, New Jersey 07961

New Mexico

Eastern New Mexico University
Child Study Clinic & Speech & Hearing Clinic
Portales, New Mexico 88130

Special Education Center
722 Silver Avenue, S.E.
Albuquerque, New Mexico

University of New Mexico
College of Education
Dept. of Education, Guidance & Counseling
Manzanita Center
Albuquerque, New Mexico

Western New Mexico University
Teacher Education Center
Department of Research
Silver City, New Mexico 19088

New Mexico Assoc. for Children with Learning Disabilities
Mrs. Virginia Bourque
1906 Amherst, N.E.
Albuquerque, New Mexico 87108

New Mexico Assoc. for Children with Learning Disabilities
Mr. Robert Granger, President
133 Sombiero Drive
Santa Fe, New Mexico 87501

New York

The Adams School
110 East 35th Street
New York, New York 10016

Brooklyn College
Dept. of Education
Educational Clinic
Brooklyn, New York 11210

Green Chimneys School
Putnam Lake Road
Brewster, New York 10509

Harlem Hospital Center
Dept. of Psychiatry
Division of Child Psychiatry
136th Street & Lenox Avenue
New York, New York 10021

Hofstra University
The Reading Center
Hempstead, New York 11550

Ithaca College
Dept. of Speech Pathology & Audiology
Sir Alexander Ewing Speech & Hearing Clinic
Ithaca, New York

The Karafin Education Center
153 Main Street
Mt. Kisco, New York

Lake Grove School
Moriches Road
Lake Grove, New York

The Lorge School
301 East 52nd Street
New York, New York

Maimonides Medical Center
Community Mental Health Center
Dept. of Child Psychiatry Services & Learning
4802 10th Avenue
Brooklyn, New York 11219

Maimonides School
34-01 Mott Avenue
Far Rockaway, New York

New York Medical College
Center for Mental Retardation
1249 5th Avenue
New York, New York 10029

New York University
Bellevue Medical Center
Dept. of Neurology & Psychiatry
Language Research Unit
550 1st Avenue
New York, New York

Psychological Consultation Center
Dept. of Psychology
525 W. 120th Street
New York, New York

Queens College
Dept. of Education
Educational Clinic
Kissetta Blvd.
Flushing, New York 11367

Rochester Institute of Technology
Counseling Center
Reading & Study Clinic
P. O. Box 3405
Rochester, New York 14614

St. Agnes Hospital
Children's Rehabilitation Center
North Street
White Plains, New York

St. Vincent's Hospital & Medical Center of New York
Dept. of Rehabilitation Medicine
153 W. 11th Street
New York, New York

State University College
Dept. of Education
Reading Center
Fredonia, New York

Stephen Gaynor School
22 W. 74th Street
New York, New York 10023

Student Skills Center Inc.
248 E. 31st Street
New York, New York

Student Skills Center, Inc.
72 N. Village Avenue
Long Island, New York

Study Center for Learning Disabilities
135 Wester Avenue
Albany, New York

Syracuse University
School of Education
Syracuse, New York 13210

Teachers College Reading Center
Dept. of Psychology
525 W. 120th Street
New York, New York

New York Assoc. for Brain Injured Children
Martha B. Bernard
305 Broadway
New York, New York 10007

New York Assoc. for Brain Injured Children
Mrs. Celeste Rudberg
95 Madison Avenue
New York, New York 10016

North Carolina

Duke University
Medical Center
Durham, North Carolina

North Carolina State University
Dept. of Psychology
P. O. Box 5096
Raleigh, North Carolina 27607

North Carolina Assoc. for Children with Learning Disabilities
Mrs. Mary Hugenschnidt
Cherry Lane Farm
Rt. 2 Box 82B
Fletcher, North Carolina 28732

North Dakota

Minot State College
Dept. of Special Education
Speech & Hearing Clinic
Minot, North Dakota 58701

University of North Dakota
Evaluation Center for Exceptional Children
Grand Forks, North Dakota

North Dakota Assoc. for Children with Learning Disabilities
Mrs. R. A. Johnson
210 South 7th
Moorhead, Minnesota 56560

North Dakota Assoc. for Children with Learning Disabilities
% Mrs. Richard Estes, President
P. O. Box #36
Christine, North Dakota 58015

Ohio

Barney Children's Medical Center
1735 Chapel Street
Dayton, Ohio 45404

Bowling Green State University
The Reading Center
301 Hanna Hall
Bowling Green, Ohio 43402

Cleveland Metropolitan General Hospital
Dept. of Pediatrics
3395 Scranton Road
Cleveland, Ohio

Kent State University
College of Education
Educational Child Study Center
Kent, Ohio 44240

Ohio State University
Dept. of Psychology
Child Study Center
65 S. Oval Drive
Columbus, Ohio 43210

Ohio University
Center for Psychological Services
McKee House
Athens, Ohio

Otterbein College
Educational Development Laboratory
Westerville, Ohio

The University of Akron
Department of Speech
Speech & Hearing Clinic
222 James Street
Akron, Ohio 44304

University Hospitals
Children's Unit
Hanna Pavilion
Dept. of Psychiatry
Cleveland, Ohio 44106

Ohio Assoc. for Children with Learning Disabilities
Henry Rumm
3160 Brandon
Upper Arlington, Ohio 43221

Ohio Assoc. for Children with Learning Disabilities
Mrs. Dale French
2738 Poplar Drive
Springfield, Ohio 45501

Oklahoma

Payne County Guidance Center
Payne County Health Dept.
701 S. Walnut
P.O. Box 471
Stillwater, Oklahoma

Tulsa Education Foundation, Inc.
1516 S. Quaker
Tulsa, Oklahoma

University of Oklahoma Medical Center
Dept. of Pediatrics
Child Study Center
601 N.E. 18th Street
Oklahoma City, Oklahoma

Community Speech & Hearing Center
University Station
Box 2262
Enid, Oklahoma

Oklahoma Assoc. for Children with Learning Disabilities
George Sevier
3408 Oklahoma
Muskogee, Oklahoma 77401

Central Oklahoma Council Assoc. for Children with Learning
    Disabilities
Mrs. Jeanne Asher
3701 N.W. 62nd Street
Oklahoma City, Oklahoma 73112

Oregon

Oregon College of Education
Dept. of Special Education & Rehabilitation
Education Evaluation Center
Monmouth, Oregon

Oregon State University
Dept. of Speech
Speech & Hearing Clinic
Corvallis, Oregon 97331

University of Oregon
School of Education
DeBusk Memorial Center
Eugene, Oregon

Willamette University
Dept. of Psychology
Salem, Oregon

University of Oregon Medical School
Crippled Children's Division
Dept. of Speech & Hearing
3181 S.W. Sam Jackson Park Road
Portland, Oregon 97201

Oregon Assoc. for Children with Learning Disabilities
Geneva Winkel, President
Portland State University Special Education
P.O. Box #751
Portland, Oregon 97207

Pennsylvania

Albert Einstein Medical Center
Dept. of Child Psychiatry
Tabor & Old York Roads
Philadelphia, Pennsylvania 19141

Bloomsburg State College
Dept. of Speech Correction
Communication Disorders
Bloomsburg, Pennsylvania

Children's Hospital of Philadelphia
Rehabilitation Dept.
1740 Bainbridge Street
Philadelphia, Pennsylvania 19146

Children's Hospital of Pittsburgh
Speech Clinic
DeSoto Street
Pittsburgh, Pennsylvania 15213

The Devereux Foundation
19 S. Waterloo Road
Devon, Pennsylvania

Edinboro State College
Dept. of Psychology & Special Education
Leader Clinic
Edinboro, Pennsylvania 16412

Episcopal Hospital
Dept. of Physical Medicine & Rehabilitation
Front Street and Lehigh Avenue
Philadelphia, Pennsylvania

Indiana University of Pennsylvania
Dept. of Special Education & Clinical Services
Campus Laboratory School
Indiana, Pennsylvania 15701

Institute of the Pennsylvania Hospitals
Dept. of Psychology & Re-education
111 N. 49th Street
Philadelphia, Pennsylvania

Laughlen Children's Center
Broad & Frederick Streets
Seweckley, Pennsylvania

Main Line Day School & Reading Center
527 E. Lancaster Avenue
St. Davids, Pennsylvania

The Matthews School
2001 Pennsylvania Avenue
Fort Washington, Pennsylvania 19034

Mercy Hospital
Division of Psychology
Audiology, Speech, & Psychology Clinic
Locust Street
Pittsburgh, Pennsylvania

Millersville State College
Dept. of Education
Reading Clinic
Millersville, Pennsylvania 17551

Muhlenberg College
Dept. of Psychology
Counseling & Guidance Clinic
Allentown, Pennsylvania

The Pathway School
Box 181
Norristown, Pennsylvania 19404

Pennsylvania College of Optometry
Dept. of Clinics
6100 N. 12th Street
Philadelphia, Pennsylvania

Pennsylvania Hospital Community Mental Health Center
Dept. of Medicine
8th & Spruce Streets
Philadelphia, Pennsylvania 19107

Pittsburgh Child Guidance Center
201 DeSoto Street
Pittsburgh, Pennsylvania 15213

School Psychology Center
Dept. of Special Education
119 E. PC II
University Park, Pennsylvania

Shippensburg State College
Dept. of Education & Psychology, Clinical Services
Shippensburg, Pennsylvania 17257

Slippery Rock State College Experimental School for Exceptional
    Children
Dept. of Special Education
Slippery Rock State College
Slippery Rock, Pennsylvania 16057

Temple University
Laboratory School of the Reading Clinic
Cheltenham & Sedgwick Avenues
Philadelphia, Pennsylvania 19150

Temple University
Dept. of Psychology
The Reading Clinic
Carnell Hall
Broad Street & Montgomery Avenue
Philadelphia, Pennsylvania 19122

University of Pennsylvania
Graduate School of Education
Reading Clinic
3700 Walnut Street
Philadelphia, Pennsylvania 19104

Vanguard School
Box 277
Haverford, Pennsylvania 19041

Westchester State College
Dept. of Speech & Theater
Speech & Hearing Clinic
620 S. High Street
Westchester, Pennsylvania

Pennsylvania Assoc. for Children with Learning Disabilities
Mrs. Leon Lock
Box 664
Allentown, Pennsylvania 18105

Pennsylvania Assoc. for Children with Learning Disabilities
2200 Brownville Road
Pittsburgh, Pennsylvania 15201

Rhode Island

Governor Center School
293 Governor Street
Providence, Rhode Island 02906

University of Rhode Island
Dept. of Education
Reading Center
Kingston, Rhode Island 02881

Rhode Island Assoc. for Children with Learning Disabilities
Mrs. Donald Levine
P.O. Box 6685
Providence, Rhode Island 02904

Rhode Island Assoc. for Children with Learning Disabilities
Dr. Charles E. Millard, President
1180 Hope Street
Bristol, Rhode Island 02809

South Carolina

University of South Carolina
School of Education
Reading Clinic
Columbia, South Carolina 29208

South Carolina Assoc. for Children with Learning Disabilities
Mrs. Gilbert LeMay
1256 Winchester
Charleston, South Carolina 29407

South Dakota

Augustana College
Crippled Children's Hospital & School
Dept. of Speech Education
Sioux Falls, South Dakota

University of South Dakota
Dept. of Speech
Speech & Hearing Clinic
Vermillion, South Dakota 57069

South Dakota Assoc. for Children with Learning Disabilities
Dr. James King
809 Kansas City Street
Rapid City, South Dakota 57401

South Dakota Assoc. for Children with Learning Disabilities
Dr. Irwin Kuske
Northern State College
Aberdeen, South Dakota 57401

Tennessee

The Bill Wilkerson Hearing & Speech Center
1114 19th Avenue South
Nashville, Tennessee

East Tennessee State University
Dept. of Special Education
Johnson City, Tennessee 37601

Memphis Speech & Hearing Center
807 Jefferson Avenue
Memphis, Tennessee 38105

Peabody College
Child Study Center
Box 158
Nashville, Tennessee

Southern College of Optometry
Dept. of Vision Training
1245 Madison
Memphis, Tennessee 38104

Tennessee Technological University
Dept. of Educational Psychology & Guidance
Counseling Center
Human Development Laboratory
Cookeville, Tennessee 38501

University of Tennessee
Dept. of Curriculum & Instruction
College of Education
Reading Center
Knoxville, Tennessee

Tennessee Oak Ridge Assoc. for Children with Learning
     Disabilities
Mrs. James Hobbs, President
Oak Ridge Schools
P.O. Box Q
Oak Ridge, Tennessee 37830

Texas

Abilene Christian College
Dept. of Speech
Station ACC
Abilene, Texas 79601

Stephen F. Austin
P.O. Box 6160
Nacogdoches, Texas

Baylor University
Office of Testing
131 Burleson Hall
Waco, Texas

Edgemoor School
2711 Fountain View
Houston, Texas

Our Lady of the Lake College
Harry Jersig Speech & Hearing Center
411 S.W. 24th Street
San Antonio, Texas 78207

Houston Speech & Hearing Center
1343 Moursund
Houston, Texas 77025

Southern Methodist University
Dept. of Education
Reading Clinic
Dallas, Texas 75222

Southwest Texas State College
San Marcos, Texas 78666

Texas Woman's University Institute for Mental & Physical
    Development
Drawer E
TWU Station
Denton, Texas

University of Texas
Dept. of Pediatrics
Medical Branch
Child Development Clinic
Galveston, Texas 77550

University of Texas
College of Education
Learning Disabilities Center
Austin, Texas 78712

University of Texas
Medical Branch
Dept. of Neurology & Psychiatry
Division of Child Psychiatry
Galveston, Texas

West Texas State University
Dept. of Speech, Education & Psychology
Canyon, Texas 79016

Texas Assoc. for Children with Learning Disabilities
Joseph B. Hall
804 Briarwood Blvd.
Arlington, Texas 76010

Texas Assoc. for Children with Learning Disabilities
Mrs. Virginia Kurko
6012 Wiesen Avenue
Fort Worth, Texas 76133

Utah

Brigham Young University
Education Center
120 College Hall, BYU
Provo, Utah

Northern Utah Mental Health Clinic
160 N. Main Street
Logan, Utah

University of Utah
Speech & Hearing Center
1699 E. 5th Street South
Salt Lake City, Utah

Youth Center
Utah State Hospital
Provo, Utah

Utah Assoc. for Children with Learning Disabilities
Marlys Anderson
3788 Brockbank Drive
Salt Lake City, Utah 84117

Vermont

Children's Rehabilitation Center of the Vermont Assoc. for the
    Crippled, Inc.
88 Park Street
P.O. Drawer 834
Rutland, Vermont 05701

DeGoesbriand Memorial Hospital
Center for Disorders of Communication
Burlington, Vermont

Overlake Day School
545 S. Prospect Street
Burlington, Vermont

United Counseling Service of Bennington County, Inc.
Dewey Street
Bennington, Vermont

Vermont Assoc. for Children with Learning Disabilities
% Miss Loretta Bergen, President
Box #131-A
Perkinsville, Vermont 05151

Virgin Islands

Virgin Islands Assoc. for Children with Learning Disabilities
Mrs. Ilse-Maria Moorehead
P.O. Box 3668
Charlotte-Amalie
St. Thomas, Virgin Islands 00801

Virginia

Glagdin School & Camp, Inc.
Box 143, Route 4
Leesburg, Virginia

Medical College of Virginia
Dept. of Neurology
Seizure Central Clinic
1200 East Broad Street
Richmond, Virginia

Old Dominion College
School of Education
Child Study Center
Hampton Blvd.
Norfolk, Virginia 23508

Tidewater Rehabilitation Institute
Diagnostic Special Education School
855 W. Brambleton Avenue
Norfolk, Virginia

University of Richmond
Psychology Dept.
Center for Psychological Services
P.O. Box 38
Richmond, Virginia 23173

University of Virginia
Speech & Hearing Center
Dept. of Speech Pathology & Audiology
109 Cabell Hall
Charlottesville, Virginia 22903

Virginia Assoc. for Children with Learning Disabilities
Dr. Eleanore Westhead
P.O. Box 5651
Charlottesville, Virginia 22901

Virginia Assoc. for Children with Learning Disabilities
Mrs. Carol Graham, President
6002 Jan Mar Drive
Falls Church, Virginia 22041

Washington

Children's Orthopedic Hospital & Medical Center
Retarded Children's Clinic
4800 Sand Point Way, N.E.
Seattle, Washington 98105

Marian School
Fort Wright College
Spokane, Washington 99204

Seattle Seguin School
113 Madrona Place, East
Seattle, Washington

Speech & Hearing Clinic
Dept. of Speech
Speech Correction
E.W.S.E.
Cheney, Washington

University of Washington
Dept. Of Pediatrics
Division of Child Health
Child Development Program
4701 24th Street, N.E.
Seattle, Washington

Washington Assoc. for Children with Learning Disabilities
Vern Bendixson
9222 183rd Place, S.W.
Edmonds, Washington 98020

Washington Assoc. for Children with Learning Disabilities
Mrs. Constance MacDonald, President
P.O. Box 1501
Wallingford Station
Seattle, Washington 98103

West Virginia

West Virginia University
Division of Clinical Studies
Child Study Center
Morgantown, West Virginia

West Virginia Assoc. for Children with Learning Disabilities
c/o Mrs. Mark Schaul, President
1551 Hampton Road
Charleston, West Virginia 25314

Wisconsin

The Cardinal Stritch College
Graduate Division
Reading Clinic
6801 N. Yates Road
Milwaukee, Wisconsin 53217

Marquette University
Dept. of Speech
Speech & Hearing Rehabilitation Center
1317 W. Wisconsin Avenue
Milwaukee, Wisconsin

Speech & Hearing Rehabilitation Center
Dept. of Communicative Disorders
905 University Avenue
Madison, Wisconsin

University of Wisconsin
Milwaukee Branch
Dept. of Education Psychology
Psycho-Educational Clinic
2513 E. Hartford Avenue
Milwaukee, Wisconsin

University of Wisconsin
Milwaukee Branch
Dept. of Exceptional Education
Special Learning Disabilities Laboratory
Milwaukee, Wisconsin

Wisconsin State University
Dept. of Speech Pathology & Audiology
Speech & Hearing Clinic
Stevens Point, Wisconsin

Wisconsin Society for Brain-Injured Children
Eli Tash
4628 N. 70 Street
Milwaukee, Wisconsin 53218

Wisconsin Assoc. for Children with Learning Disabilities
Gary L. Griffin, President
P.O. Box #184
Appleton, Wisconsin 54911

Appendix B

Where to Learn More about Hyperactivity: A Bibliography

Adler, Sidney J., and Keith C. Terry, *Your Overactive Child: Normal or Not?* New York: Medcom Press, 1972.

Alabiso, Frank, "Inhibitory Functions of Attention in Reducing Hyperactive Behavior," *American Journal of Mental Deficiency*, 77:3, 1972, 259-282.

Arnold, L. Eugene, "The Art of Medicating Hyperkinetic Children," *Clinical Pediatrics*, 12:1, (January 1973), 35-41.

Arnold, L. Eugene, Donald Strobl, and Allen Weisenberg, "Hyperkinetic Adult," JAMA, 222:6, (Nov. 6, 1972), 693-694.

Auerbach, Aaron G., "The Social Control of Learning Disabilities," *Journal of Learning Disabilities*, Aug-September 1971.

Bazell, Robert J., "Panel Sanctions Amphetamines for Hyperkinetic Children," *Science* 171 (3977):1223, March 26, 1971.

Beck, Joan, *Minimal Brain Dysfunction*, CANHC, P.O. Box 604, Los Angeles, Ca. 90053, 1970.

Brown, P., and R. Elliott, "Control of Aggression in a Nursery School Class," *Journal of Exceptional Child Psychiatry*, 2, (1965), 103-107.

Burks, H. F., "Effects of Amphetamine Therapy on Hyperkinetic Children," *Archives of General Psychiatry*, 11, (1965), 604-609.

Buscaglia, Leo F., *Love as A Behavior Modifier, and Help Me! I Have An Exceptional Child*. Texas Association for Children with Learning Disabilities, 1971.

CANHC-GRAM, The official newsletter of the California Association for Neurologically Handicapped Children. P.O. Box 604, Los Angeles, Ca. 90053.

Carpenter, Robert D., *Dear Doctor* . . . . . RDC Publishers, P.O. Box 1817, Whittier, Ca. 90609.

Clements, Sam D., *Minimal Brain Dysfunction in Children*, NINDB Monograph No. 3, Public Health Service Publication No. 1415, Section 6, U.S. Department of Health, Education and Welfare, Washington, D.C., 1966.

Clements, Sam D., and Laura E. Lehtinen, *Children with Minimal Brain Injury: A Symposium*. National Society for Crippled Children and Adults, Chicago, Ill. 1963.

Cochran, E. V., *Teach and Reach That Child*. Peck Publications, 4067 Transport St., Palo Alto, Ca. (1971). Especially designed for teachers.

Conners, C. K., "Recent Drug Studies with Hyperkinetic Children," *Journal of Learning Disabilities*, 4:9, November, 1971.

Cruickshank, William M., *The Brain Injured Child in Home, School, and Community*. New York; Syracuse: Syracuse U. Press, 1967.

Cruickshank, William M., *A Teaching Method For Brain Injured and Hyperactive Children*. Syracuse; Syracuse University Press, 1971.

Dunn, L. M., *Peabody Picture Vocabulary Test*. Minneapolis; American Guidance Service, 1959.

Ebersole, Marylou, Newell C. Kephart, and James B. Ebersole, *Steps to Achievement for the Slow Learner*. Charles E. Merrill Publishing Co., Columbus, Ohio, 1968.

Epps, Helen O., *Teaching Devices for Children with Impaired Learning*. Parents Volunteer Association of the Columbus State Schools, Inc., Columbus, Ohio, 1964.

The Exceptional Parent. P.O. Box 101, Back Bay Annex, Boston, Mass. 02117. Offers practical guidance for parents of children with disabilities. Published six times per year.

Frierson, Edward G., and Walter B. Barbe, *Educating Children with Learning Disabilities: Selected Readings.* New York: Appleton-Century-Crofts, 1967.

Golick, Margaret, *She Thought I was Dumb but I told Her I Had A . . . Learning Disability.* Canadian Broadcasting Corp. Toronto, 1969.

Haverkamp, Leona J., "Brain Injured Children and the School Nurse," *The Journal of School Health*, May, 1970.

Hentoff, Nat, "The Drugged Classroom," *Evergreen Review* (December 1970).

Johnson, Doris J., "Educational Principles for Children with Learning Disabilities," *Rehabilitation Literature*, 38:10, (October 1967), 317-322.

Kappelman, Murray M., Alfred B. Rosenstein, and Robert L. Ganter, "Comparison of Disadvantaged Children With Learning Disabilities and Their Successful Peer Group," *American Journal of the Disabled Child*, 124 (December 1972), 875-879.

Kershner, John R., "Anxiety and Hyperactivity in Learning Disabilities." Paper presented at the Indiana University Sesquicentennial Symposium on the Relationship of Emotional and Motor Domains, Bloomington, May 1970.

Krippner, Stanley, Robert Silverman, Michael Cavallo, and Michael Healy, "A Study of hyperkinetic Children Receiving Stimulant Drugs," *Academic Therapy* 8:3, (Spring 1973), 261-269.

Ladd, E. T., "Pills for Classroom Peace?" *Saturday Review*, November 21, 1970).

Laufer, Maurice W., "Long Term Management and Some Follow-up Findings On The Use of Drugs with Minimal Cerebral Syndromes, *Journal of Learning Disabilities*, 4:9 (November 1971), 519-522.

Learning Disorders in Children, Report of the First Ross Conference on Pediatric Research, pub. by Ross Laboratories, Columbus, Ohio 43216.

McNamar, John J., "Hyperactivity in the Apartment Bound Child," *Clinical Pediatrics* (July 1972), 371-372.

Mendelson, Wallace, Noel Johnson, and Mark A. Stewart, "Hyperactive Children as Teenagers: A Follow-up Study," *The Journal of Nervous and Mental Disease*, 153:4, 273-279.

Minde, K., *A Parents' Guide To Hyperactivity in Children.* Quebec Association for Children with Learning Disabilities. 6338 Victoria Ave., Montreal 252, Quebec, Canada, 1971.

Minde, K., and G. Webb, "Studies on the Hyperactive Child: Paranatal Factors Associated with Hyperactivity." *Developmental Medicine In Child Neurology*, in press.

Morrison, J. R., and M. A. Steward, "A Family Study of the Hyperactive Child Syndrome," *Biol. Psychiat.*, 3, 1971, 189-197.

National Society for Crippled Children and Adults, 2023 W. Ogden Ave., Chicago, Ill. 60612. Will send free packet of information about minimal brain dysfunction.

Nelson, C. Donald, "Subtle Brain Damage: Its Influence on Listening and Language," *Elementary School Journal*, March, 1961.

Quitkin, F., and D. F. Klein, "Two Behavioral Syndromes in Young Adults Related to Possible Minimal Brain Dysfunction," *Journal of Psychiatric Residence*, 7, (1969), 131-142.

"Report of the Conference on the Use of Stimulant Drugs in the Treatment of Behaviorally Disturbed Young School Children," sponsored by the Office of Child Development and the Office of the Assistant Secretary for Health and Scientific Affairs, Department of Health, Education, and Welfare, Washington, D.C., January, 1971.

Rice, Ruth Dianne, "Educo-Therapy: A New Approach to Delinquent Behavior," *Journal of Learning Disabilities*, 3:1 (January 1970), 18-23.

Smith, Lendon H., "The Hypermotor Child," In *The Children's Doctor*. Englewood Cliffs: Prentice-Hall, Inc., 1969, 77-92.

Stewart, Mark A., "Hyperactive Children," *Scientific American*, 222:4 (April 1970), 94-99.

Stewart, Mark, and S. Olds, *Raising the Hyperactive Child*. New York: Harper and Row, 1973.

Tarnopol, Lester, "Delinquency and Minimal Brain Dysfunction," *Journal of Learning Disabilities*, 3:4 (April 1970), 200-207.

Thompson, Alice C., *Educationally Handicapped: A Handbook for Teachers*. California State College at Los Angeles, 1966.

Van Witsen, Betty, *Perceptual Training Activities Handbook*. Teachers College Press, Columbia U., New York, 1972.

Wender, Paul H., *Minimal Brain Dysfunction in Children*, Wiley-Interscience, New York, 1971.

Appendix C

Glossary

Aggressive

Many hyperactive children have what psychiatrists and psychologists call "unsocialized *aggressive* disorder of childhood." This means the hyperactive child may be over-anxious, hostile, and disruptive at home or at school.

Allergy

A state of unusual sensitivity to certain substances, toxins, and allergens. Many children manifest allergy in association with hyperactivity. They may have asthma, skin conditions, runny noses, and "frequent colds." The hyperactivity may be increased by the underlying allergy.

Amino acids

Any of a group of complex organic compounds of nitrogen that combine in various ways to form proteins. Although the amino acids are generally normal in hyperactive children, some of the amino acid disorders such as PKU may have hyperactive behavior or autistic symptoms which are in association with high levels of phenylalanine in the blood.

Amphetamine drugs

These are drugs such as dextroamphetamine and related compounds, such as Ritalin® (methylphenidate), which are mood elevators or stimulants of the central nervous system which may have an opposite effect on the hyperactive child by calming him and modifying his behavior, probably related to the chemical mediators or inhibitory pathways of the brain.

Anemia

This is a blood condition caused by insufficiency of the red blood corpuscles. Most hyperactive children have a normal blood count. Very low blood counts that cause severe anemia may result in either lethargy or irritability.

Antihistamines

These are drugs which inhibit histamine or allergic responses. Some of the antihistamines, such as Benadryl®, may have a relaxing effect on certain hyperactive children, as well as helping their allergic reactions.

Anxiety

Uneasy, tense feelings, thoughts, or fears. Many hyperactive children are immature and have anxiety over new situations and classroom experiences.

Articulation

The way of speaking. Many hyperactive children have articulation disorders in speech and communication, with slurring, stuttering, and difficulty in pronunciation.

Ataxia

Refers to abnormal body coordination that may cause the patient to walk in a drunken manner. It is due to cerebellar brain dysfunction. Generally, hyperactive children are normal in cerebellar function, and their incoordination is due to minimal dysfunction in the cerebral cortex rather than the cerebellum.

Audiologist

An expert who tests hearing and perception and prescribes hearing aids. Most hyperactive children have normal hearing, but may have poor auditory perception.

Auditory

Having to do with the organs of hearing, the eighth cranial nerve.

Auditory perception

A brain function whereby meaning is acquired from sound. Many hyperactive children have auditory perceptual disorders.

Autistic

An unusual behavior manifestation with loss of contact in the environment, manifested by twirling, whirling, poor eye contact and communication. The autistic child may have speech problems and hyperactive behavior.

Cerebral palsy

A brain dysfunction causing motor abnormalities, such as spasticity, weakness, incoordination due to athetosis (basal ganglia), or cerebellar dysfunction. There are many types of cerebral palsy, such as weakness on one side, weakness on two sides, three sides, or four sides associated with speech problems and mental retardation and other physical handicaps. Many cerebral palsy children are hyperactive due to their brain dysfunction on a neurological basis.

Chromosome

The genetic material found in the

nucleus of all cells. There are 46 human chromosomes. The chromosome karyotype and composition are normal in the hyperactive child. Certain chromosomal disorders, such as an extra chromosome in the Y group, called the XYY, are said to have hyperactive and aggressive behavior. Others, as an extra X in the XXY, or Klinefelter's syndrome, may have aggressive or hypoactive behavior, depending on the age and environmental influence of the child. In missing chromosomes, such as XO or Turner's syndrome, there may be other emotional, behavioral, and perceptual difficulties. In other chromosomal abnormalities with increasing number or missing chromosomes or deletions or translocations, there may be behavioral changes, but this may be associated with mental retardation and other brain and organ dysfunctions.

Diabetes   A metabolic disorder with clinical manifestations of lethargy, increased thirst (polydipsia), increased appetite (polyphagia), weakness, dry skin, and weight loss. The blood sugar is high. The beta cells of the pancreas are not secreting enough insulin, which has multiple clinical effects on the body.

Dysfunction   Any impairment or abnormality in the body or organ systems.

Dysgraphia   Abnormality in handwriting. Many hyperactive children have difficulty in spatial orientation, figure-ground, position sense, which may affect brain function or putting letters together, seeing spaces between words, and other abnormalities in arrangement.

Electroenceph-alogram
A tracing made by the encephalograph machine which records surface potentials on the scalp from the underlying brain activity. Some hyperactive children show abnormalities such as spiking, or slowing of the waves. The electroencephalogram detects brain damage, epilepsy or seizure disorders, and space-occupying lesions.

Ephedrines
Drugs related to the amphetamines which may stimulate the central nervous system in certain individuals, or act as decongestants.

Episodic
Repeated, recurring, related and integrated incidents. This is important to the doctor in diagnosing seizure disorders as some hyperactive children may have episodic behavioral reactions which may be related to metabolic dysfunction or brain dysfunction.

Functional
Psychiatrists use "functional" as meaning a psychological basis for the problem, while "organic" means it is due to some brain dysfunction.

Gait
A way of walking or running. Many hyperactive children may have gait disturbances due to their minimal incoordination.

Gene
A minute part of the chromosome that controls enzymes which in turn control metabolic function. A gene may control inheritance and development. The relationship of genes to the hyperactive syndrome is still under investigation.

Genetic	This relates to cytogenetic, chromosomes, and heredity. Many hyperactive children may have inherited patterns of behavior and other neurological and educational abnormalities.
Glucose tolerance test	A laboratory test to measure body responses to a carbohydrate or sugar load, detecting diabetes or hyperglycemia, and the opposite, hypoglycemia.
Histamines	Substances released by the body in allergic reactions.
Hyperplasia	A condition of increased tissue. Hyperplasia of the gums (puffy gums), may be found in children who are taking Dilantin® or other drugs.
Hyposensitization	A process to lower the body sensitivity to allergy-producing agents. The allergist may give injections of allergic substances which have been diluted to produce a lower sensitivity to the corresponding allergin.
Kinesthetic	Having to do with sensations of touch, temperature of the muscles, joints, and skin. Many hyperactive children have difficulty in two-point discrimination and kinesthetic awareness.
Kinetic	Having to do with motion. "Hyper" means above or increased, and hyperkinetic behavior is motion or movement that is above the normal. Many hyperactive children have random, purposeless, incoordinated and overactive movements.
Metabolism	The process of building up or breaking down of food substances. The metabolism of the body has multiple functions and these are controlled by genes, enzymes, and basic

substances such as proteins, sugars, and starches.

Minimal cerebral dysfunction

Another term for the hyperactive child who has a minimal clumsiness syndrome with learning and behavior problems.

Motor abilities

The effect of stimuli from the central nervous system of the motor cortex of the brain causing the muscles to function normally or abnormally.

Ophthalmologist

A medical doctor (M.D.) who specializes in the structure, function, and diseases of the eye.

Optometrist

A specialist (not an M.D.) who measures the powers of sight and tests eyes to fit them with glasses.

Perception

A brain function which receives and interprets stimuli received by the senses. The hyperactive child often has difficulty with both auditory and visual perceptions.

Psychometrist

A psychologist or person skilled in the administration and measuring of tests of a psychological nature for determining intelligence, perceptual disorders, and school and learning problems.

Psychosis

A severe form of mental disturbance or disease. Many psychotic behavioral reactions may manifest in hyperactive, bizarre behavior patterns.

Psychotherapy

The treatment of mental or emotional disorders through psychological techniques. It is given by physicians, psychologists, speech therapists, educational therapists, teachers, as supportive, suggestive, analytic, and remedial techniques.

Psychotropic agents	These are drugs that affect brain function. Some are mood elevators, others are depressants.
Remediation	The process of working to improve study habits, skills, and correction of educational and behavioral problems. The hyperactive child may have associated learning problems which need remediation in special classes, as in educationally handicapped classes or privately with an educational therapist.
Rorschach test	A test for determining personality traits based on a subject's response to set ink block designs. Its use is not routine but it is employed when psychologists and psychiatrists seek a more in-depth analysis of personality.
Schizophrenia	A mental disorder in which the patient is disassociated from his environment and self. *Schizo* means split, and *phrenia* means brain. Childhood schizophrenia may be characterized by impulsiveness and hyperactivity. The term has other clinical characteristics not associated with the purely hyperkinetic behavior.
Stimulus	Something that excites an organ or part of the body, causing it to react. Many hyperactive children are overstimulated by the normal stimuli of the environment and they over-react.
Syndrome	A group of signs or symptoms considered together. Examples are the hyperactive behavior syndrome which may consist of the impulse disorder, as well as the motor and mental abnormalities which can also be called the minimal clumsiness syndrome or

the minimal cerebral dysfunction syndrome.

Tactile   Having to do with the sensation of touch. Hyperactive children may have abnormalities in tactile kinesthetic sensation.

Temporal lobes   The side portion of the brain having to do with behavioral functions.

Visual acuity   Refers to how the child sees. The hyperactive child has normal visual acuity for the most part and although he may have reading problems, his vision and eye refraction are normal.

Visual perception   A brain function whereby meaning is acquired from what one sees. Many hyperactive children have visual perceptual disorders.

Appendix D
Sample Forms
and Questionnaires

The following forms and questionnaires are the ones I use in my clinic. The specialist to whom you take your child will probably have similar forms and tests. By studying the material that follows, you will get a better idea of what to expect when you take your child in for treatment.

CLINIC FORMS
Neurological Evaluation

<u>GROWTH AND DEVELOPMENT FORM</u>

I. FAMILY HISTORY (please circle items which are
                    true and give details on
                    reverse side)

Mental Retardation	Growth Problems
Mental Illness	Heart Disease
Emotional Problems	Kidney Disease
Schizophrenia	Liver Disease
Seizures	Allergy
Headaches	Blindness
Cataracts	Asthma
Hearing Problems	Hyperactivity
Diabetes	Behavior Problem
Thyroid Disorder	School Problem

Has the mother or father had any serious medical problem?

_____

How many brothers?_____ Have they had any medical problems?

_____

How many sisters?_____ Have they had any medical problems?

_____

Have there been any miscarriages?___ If yes, please explain

_____

II. PREGNANCY (please circle if any of the below
               occurred during pregnancy)

Nausea	Dizziness
Vomiting	Fever
Bleeding	Swelling
Infections	X-rays
High Blood Pressure	German Measles
Headaches	Flu
Blurry Vision	Other viruses

         Please give details on other side

How much weight did you gain in pregnancy?_____
What medications did you take during pregnancy?_____

_____

Was your baby on time?_____ If not, please state early or
late and how many weeks?_____
How long was your labor?_____
Were there any complications?_____
Were there any complications during delivery?_____

III. NEWBORN HISTORY

Father's age at time of delivery_____

Mother's age at time of delivery_____

Birth weight of baby_____ Length of baby_____

Head circumference_____ Were there any complications
or problems at or after birth?_____

If yes, please explain in detail_____

_____

Where was baby born?_____

IV. GROWTH AND DEVELOPMENT

At what age did baby hold up his head?_____ Sit up_____

Stand up while holding on_____ Walk_____ Crawl_____

Ride a tricycle_____ Drink from a cup_____

At what age did he help in self care and feed himself____

At what age was he bowel trained____ Bladder trained_____

What age was he when he had his first tooth_____

What hand does he write with_____

What foot does he kick the ball with_____

Please circle the following if it is a problem:

      Poor Coordination   Social
      Speech   Reading
      Growth   Writing
      Learning   Arithmetic
      School   Spelling

Please circle if the child has had:

      Whooping Cough   Mumps
      Chicken Pox   Measles
      Pneumonia   Rheumatic Fever
      Scarlet Fever   Polio
      Encephalitis   German Measles
      Meningitis

Has your child had any surgeries?_____ If so, please
explain. Include what was done, the year, and the hospital

_____

_____

_____

_____

Has your child had any seizures, spells, fits, or epilepsy?

_____

Did your child have a speech problem in the past or present?_____

_____

Please indicate names and addresses of other physicians that this child has seen in the past:

    Name   Date   Reason

_____

_____

_____

_____

_____

What school does this child attend?_____
Address_____
Present teacher_____
How is he doing in school?_____
Please ask his teacher for a report on his progress.
This is very important

Who referred you to our center?

Name_____
Address_____ Telephone #_____
Do you want us to mail a report to them? Yes_____ No_____

THANK YOU FOR COMPLETING THIS FORM. YOUR THOUGHTFULNESS
WILL AID US IN GIVING YOUR CHILD THE BEST POSSIBLE CARE
HERE AT DIVISION MEDICAL.

Seizure Questionnaire

(Fits, Convulsions, Attacks, Spélls & Epilepsy)

Name_____ Date/Birth_____ Age_____ Sex__M __F

This questionnaire is to be filled out as completely as possible to help the doctor evaluate your child.

I. Please <u>circle</u>, if YES:

   1. Eyes rolling
   2. Breath holding
   3. Tongue biting
   4. Respiration
   5. Generalized stiffness
   6. One-sided stiffness
   7. Headaches
   8. Abdominal Pains
   9. Behavior abnormal-- before   after
   10. Falling
   11. Unconsciousness
   12. Fever, convulsions
   13. Staring spells

II. HISTORY OF ACCIDENT (If yes, describe on back)

   1. Head injury:_____Yes ___No
   2. Meningitis:_____Yes ___No
   3. Encephalitis:_____Yes ___No
   4. Brain tumor:_____Yes ___No
   5. Dehydration:_____Yes ___No
   6. Hypoglycemia:_____Yes ___No
   7. Birth injury:_____Yes ___No

III. MEDICATION

Types	Amt. & Dosage	Times/day	Date Started	Date Stopped
1.				
2.				
3.				
4.				

IV. When was the first Seizure?_____

Please describe in detail_____

_____

When was the last Seizure?_____

Please describe in detail_____

_____

How often do they occur?_____

Who in the family has seizures?_____

Migraine Headaches?_____

V.   HISTORY OF: Circle if Yes and describe in detail in back

   1. Emotional problems
   2. School problems

123

        3. Hearing problems
        4. Visual problems
        5. Mental retardation

VI. Describe every detail of a typical seizure, spell, or
     attack on the back of this page.

Headache Questionnaire

Name_____ Age_____ Date_____

Check if associated with headache

_____ Irritability
_____ Depression
_____ Frequent Urination
_____ Vomiting
_____ Nausea
_____ Numbness
_____ Visual Disturbance
_____ Pains in other parts of body
_____ Pains when combing hair
_____ Pain on moving head
_____ Cavities (teeth)
_____ Poor appetite
_____ Head injury
_____ Dizziness
_____ Clumsiness
_____ Confusion
_____ Loss of consciousness
_____ Difficulty sleeping
_____ Swallowing
_____ Neck injury
_____ Sleep after headache
_____ Behavior change with or after headache

1. When did your headache start?_____
   (month and year)

2. How often do you get headaches?_____

3. When does headache occur? .....morning...noon...night
   ...after meals...before meals... (circle)

4. What medicine do you take for your headaches?_____
   _____

5. Does medicine help headache?_____

6. What medicines have you tried?_____

7. What medications are you taking regularly beside the
   above?_____

8. Who else in your family has headaches?_____
   How long?_____ What diagnosis?_____

9. Where on your head does headache occur? (circle)
   front side back   neck all over   right   left

10. Describe your headache_____
    Sudden   Throbbing   Pulsating Tight (band-like)
    Steady ache   Sharp   Pressure   (circle)

11. How long does your headache last?_____
    With medication_____ Without medication_____

125

Dizziness Questionnaire

Is your dizziness constant?_____ Or in attacks?_____

Part A:

1. Do you lose your balance when walking?   Yes__ No__
                to the left?_____
                to the right?_____

2. Do you have headaches?   Yes__ No__
   If yes, ask for headache questionnaire.

3. Problems pertaining to your ears (circle).
   a. Ear pain?   Rt. Lt.
   b. Discharge from your ears?   Rt. Lt.
   c. Fullness or stuffiness in your ears?   Rt. Lt.
   d. Difficulty in hearing?   Rt. Lt.
   e. Noise in ears?   Rt. Lt.
      Describe noise_____

4. Do you have double vision?   Yes__ No__
           blurred vision or blindness? Yes__ No__
           difficulty in swallowing? Yes__ No__
           difficulty in speech? Yes__ No__
           confusion? Yes__ No__
           numbness of face or extremities?
                                 Yes__ No__
           weakness in legs or arms? Yes__ No__
           allergies?_____ Yes__ No__
                (what type of allergies)

5. Did you have any head injuries?   Yes__ No__
   _____
          (if yes, give date)

6. Do you take any medications?   Yes__ No__
           for dizziness?_____ Yes__ No__
                   (what)
           for other reasons?_____ Yes__ No__
                     (what)

Part B:

I. 1. When was your first attack?_____

    2. How often do you get these attacks?

    _____

    3. How long does the attack last?_____

    4. Do you have any warning that the attack
       is about to start?   Yes__ No__

    5. Is the attack precipitated by bending
       down?   Yes__ No__

6. Is the attack worse when you close
   your eyes?   Yes___ No___

7. Do you know how to stop the attack?   Yes___ No___

   How?_____

8. Are you completely free of dizziness
   between attacks?   Yes___ No___

II. Check if attack is associated with:

1. Objects spinning or turning around you.   _____

2. Tendency to fall: to the right   _____

                      to the left   _____

                      forward   _____

                      backward   _____

3. Blacking out   _____

4. Loss of consciousness   _____

5. Headache   _____

6. Nausea and/or vomiting   _____

Behavior Checklist

Name_____ Age_____ Date_____

(Please check behavior observed.)

Oddness, bizarre behavior_____

In a world of his own, preoccupation_____

Social withdrawal_____

Fixed expression_____

Lack of emotional reaction_____

Depression_____   In School____ At Home____

Aggressiveness_____   In School____ At Home____

Hostile_____   In School____ At Home____

Disruptive_____   In School____ At Home____

Short attention span_____

Impulsive_____

Hyperactive (always on the go-can't sit still)_____

Dislike for school_____

Disruptiveness (tendency to annoy and bother others)_____

Self-consciousness (easily embarrassed)_____

Jealousy_____

Temper tantrums_____

Laziness_____   In School____ At Home____

Distractible_____

Clumsiness (awkwardness, poor muscular coordination,
            falling frequently)_____

Profanity (swearing, cursing)_____

Bed wetting (enuresis)_____

Physical complaints: Headaches____ Stomach____

                            Ulcers____ Diarrhea____

                            Frequency of urination____

                            Constipation____

Fecal soiling (soils his pants during day or night_____

Tics or other motor movements
            (involuntarily or voluntarily)_____

Stealing_____

Masturbation_____

Sexual problems_____

Others (please describe)_____

_____

128

Achievement List

TASK	POOR	AVER.	GOOD	EXC.	OUT-STAND.
1. Clearly understandable vocabulary.					
2. Vocabulary at proper age level.					
3. Able to repeat a sentence of proper length for age.					
4. Uses imagination when playing by himself.					
5. Able to build with blocks (large and small)					
6. Recognizes colors					
7. Knows basic shapes (circle, square, rectangle & triangle)					
8. Reproduces shape when asked to					
9. Draw a person.					
10. Recognizes numbers (1-10).					
11. Reproduces numerals (1-10).					
12. Recognizes letters (A-Z & a-z).					
13. Reproduces letters (A-Z & a-z).					
14. Recognizes objects and their use.					
15. Same and different.					

TASK	POOR	AVER.	GOOD	EXC.	OUT-STAND.
16. Small, smaller, smallest.					
17. Large, larger, largest.					
18. Memory (sequencing)					
19. Reading (level)					
20. Spelling (level)					
21. Understands number meaning					
22. Addition.					
23. Subtraction.					
24. Multiplication.					
25. Division.					
26. Cursive (A-Z & a-z)					
27. Reading Comprehension.					
28. Punctuation.					
29. Creative writing					
30. Grammar.					
31. Phonic Attack					
32. Phonic Consonant Sound.					
33. Phonic Vowel Sound.					
34. Phonic Blend Sound					
35. Phonic closure					

TASK	POOR	AVER.	GOOD	EXC.	OUT-STAND.
36. Self image.					
37. Responsive to praise.					
38. Responsive to negative motivation.					
39. Responsible for homework.					
40. Desire to learn.					
41. Does homework.					
42. Relates to mother.					

REMARKS:

TESTS
Description and Terminology of Tests

I. <u>DENVER DEVELOPMENTAL SCREENING TEST</u> (DDST)

    A. <u>Description</u>

       1. The Denver Developmental Screening Test was devised and standardized as a rapid, simple, clinical test to detect children with developmental retardation.

    B. <u>Procedure</u>

       1. The parent is asked questions about the child.

       2. The child is asked to perform specific tasks.

    C. <u>Diagnostic Value</u>

       1. Gross Motor Development

       2. Fine Motor Development

       3. Language

       4. Behavior

II. <u>FROSTIG DEVELOPMENTAL TEST OF VISUAL PERCEPTION</u> (FDT)

    A. <u>Description</u>

       1. The Frostig test measures eye-motor coordination, figure-ground, constancy of shape, position in space, and spatial relationships. These specific subtest results are relevant to the child's performance in nursery school, kindergarten, and the elementary years. The ability to achieve in these areas determines greatly if a child is able to reproduce and recognize the sequence of letters to form a word or sequence of words forming a sentence.

    B. <u>Procedure</u>

       1. <u>Eye-Motor Coordination</u> -- Eye-hand coordination involving the drawing of continuous, straight, curved, or angled lines between boundaries of various width, length or from one point to another point without guide lines.

       2. <u>Figure-Ground</u> -- Test shifts in perception of figures against increasingly complex grounds. Intersecting and hidden geometric forms are used.

       3. <u>Constancy of Shape</u> -- Tests recognition of certain geometric figures presented in various sizes, shadings, textures, and positions in space, and their discrimination from similar geometric figures. Circles, squares, rectangles, ellipses and parallelograms are used.

4. <u>Position in Space</u> -- Tests discrimination of reversals and rotations of figures presented in series. Schematic drawings representing common objects are used.

5. <u>Spatial Relationships</u> -- Tests analysis of simple forms and patterns. These consist of lines of various lengths and angles which the child is required to copy, using dots as guide points.

C. <u>Diagnostic Value</u>

1. Reveals exact age equivalent of visual perceptual retardation.

III. <u>DRAW A PERSON</u> (DAP)

A. <u>Description</u>

This test is not threatening to the child because it is not limited to his ability to speak, his academic achievement, his cultural, or parental deprivation.

B. <u>Procedure</u>

The child is asked to draw a figure on a sheet of paper, without mentioning an age or sex. Then the child is asked questions that could enable the child to express his emotional feelings.

C. <u>Diagnostic Value</u>

1. Body image

2. Perceptual deficits

3. Mental Age (which can be calculated to an I. Q. Score)

4. Projection of child's emotional feelings

IV. <u>WIDE RANGE ACHIEVEMENT TEST</u> (WRAT)

A. <u>Description</u>

This test is used to calculate the grade level of achievement in reading, spelling and arithmetic.

B. <u>Procedure</u>

1. The child is asked to reproduce given symbols in limited amount of space.

2. The child prints or writes his name.

3. The child is given orally a list of words to spell, in writing.

4. The child is given an oral and written arithmetic test.

5. The child is tested to see if he can relate one letter to another.

6. He is asked to read a standard word list.

133

C. Diagnostic Value
 1. Learning disabilities
    a. Dyslexia
    b. Dysgraphia
    c. Dyscalculia
 2. Grade level of achievement
    a. Reading
    b. Spelling
    c. Arithmetic
 3. Checking progress in remedial programs

V. BENDER-GESTALT TEST (BG)

A. Description

This test was established on the premise that the reproduction of test design is a visual-motor act in which distortion of original patterns indicate malfunctioning due to neural injury.

B. Procedure

The child is shown nine cards in sequence; each contains a geometric design. The child reproduces the design.

C. Diagnostic Value
 1. Disturbed muscle coordination
 2. Emotional problems
 3. Visual Perception
 4. Organicity (Brain Damage)

VI. PEABODY PICTURE VOCABULARY TEST (PPVT)

A. Description

The Peabody Picture Vocabulary Test is designed to provide an estimate of a subject's verbal intelligence through measuring his auditory vocabulary.

B. Procedure

The examiner places a book of pictures in front of the child. There are four pictures on each page. The examiner gives a word orally and the child points to one of the four pictures that represents the given word.

C. Diagnostic Value
 1. Verbal Intelligence Quotient (I.Q.)
 2. Mental Age Quotient (M.A.)

3. Auditory Reception

4. Comprehension

VII. <u>CHILDREN'S APPERCEPTION TEST</u>
(3 years to 10 years), (CAT)

<u>THEMATIC APPERCEPTION TEST</u>
(11 years through adulthood), (TAT)

A. <u>Description</u>

A method of investigating personality by studying
the dynamic meaningfulness of the individual
differences in perception of standard stimuli.

B. <u>PROCEDURE-CHILDREN'S APPERCEPTION TEST</u>

The test consists of ten pictures depicting
animals in various situations. The child studies
the picture then projects, orally, his own emotional feelings.

C. <u>Procedure-Thematic Apperception Test</u>

The test consists of twenty pictures depicting
classical human situations. The adolescent or
adult relate to the picture and project, orally,
their emotional feelings.

D. <u>Diagnostic Value-Children's Apperception Test</u>

1. Facilitates understanding of a child's
relationship

2. Presents the child's ability to verbalize

3. Releases the child's subconscious emotions

E. <u>Diagnostic Value-Thematic Apperception Test</u>

1. Reveals the dominant drives and conflicts of
personality

2. Presents the patient's ability to verbalize

3. Releases the patient's subconscious emotions

VIII. <u>SENTENCE COMPLETION</u> (SC)

A. <u>Description</u>

The child is given a paper of incomplete sentences.

B. <u>Procedure</u>

The child is asked to read and complete each
sentence. Examiner may read the sentence and
write the child's completion for the sentence,
if the child is not able to read or write.

C. <u>Diagnostic Value</u>

1. Comprehension (reading)

2. Reasoning (to reach a conclusion)

3. Penmanship
4. Spelling
5. Emotional Projection

IX. WECHSLER INTELLIGENCE SCALE FOR CHILDREN
(5 years to 15.11 years), (WISC)

WECHSLER ADULT INTELLIGENCE SCALE
(16 years to 75 years and over), (WAIS)

A. Description

These tests are both verbal and performance tests
and therefore reveal very accurate diagnosis

B. Procedure

1. Verbal (Examiner presents questions orally)

   a. Information------Example: "How many ears
      have you?"

   b. Comprehension----Example: "Why are crimin-
      als locked up?"

   c. Arithmetic-------Example: "At 7¢ each,
      what will 3 cigars cost?"

   d. Vocabulary-------Example: "What does hat
      mean?"

   e. Similarities-----Example: "In what way are
      a plum and a peach alike?"

   f. Digit Span-------Example: "Repeat digits
      forward and backward."

2. Performance

   a. Picture Arrangement--------
      Example: Arrangement of related
      pictures to form a story.

   b. Picture Completion---------
      Example: Name the important
      missing part in each of a series
      of pictures.

   c. Object assembly------------
      Example: Taking a familiar
      configuration and placing it
      into a meaningful whole.

   d. Block Design----------------
      Example: Construction of designs
      with colored blocks.

   e. Coding----------------------
      Example: Putting symbols for
      numerals according to sample.

C. Diagnostic Value

    1. Verbal

        a. Long-range retention

        b. Reasoning with abstraction

        c. Retention of arithmetic processes

        d. Language development

        e. Analysis of relationships

        f. Immediate recall

    2. Performance

        a. Visual perception of relationship

        b. Visual imagery perception

        c. Visual motor integration

        d. Perception of form

        e. Immediate visual motor integration

    3. Intelligence Quotient (Verbal, Performance and Full Quotient)

X. ILLINOIS TEST OF PSYCHOLINGUISTIC ABILITIES (ITPA)

A. Description

This test is arranged to cover the areas of Visual, Auditory, Verbal, and Manual Expression. This is given at the age of 2 years 4 months up to 10 years 3 months.

B. Procedure

    1. Visual

        a. Visual Reception

Each item is exposed for a given time limit and then the student points to one of the four alternatives that relate to the original item.

        b. Visual Sequential Memory

Student is exposed to sequence cards for 5 seconds and then asked to reproduce with chips the same sequence.

        c. Visual Association

The student is asked to point to one of four peripheral pictures which is most closely associated with a central picture.

        d. Visual Closure

Student is given 30 seconds to find given objects that are hidden within a picture.

137

2. Auditory

    a. Auditory Association

        Examiner reads the incomplete analogy, stopping abruptly without dropping his voice to indicate that the sentence is not complete. The student then supplies the final term.

    b. Auditory Sequential Memory

        Student is asked to repeat increasingly longer sequences of digits presented at a uniform rate of 2 per second.

    c. Auditory Closure

        The examiner presents each word at a normal speaking rate with the indicated sounds omitted. Student then supplies the completed word.

    d. Sound Blending

        Examiner pronounces each word by syllables and the student repeats the whole word.

3. Verbal Expression

    a. Student is asked to describe verbally 5 items.

4. Manual Expression

    a. Student is asked to demonstrate the use of the pictured objects.

C. Diagnostic Value

    1. Visual Perceptual Deficits

    2. Auditory Perceptual Deficits

    3. Psycholinguistic Age

    4. Psycholinguistic Age Norm in each subtest reveals the amount of retardation

XI. TERMINOLOGY USED IN THE DIAGNOSES OF LEARNING PROBLEMS

A. Dyslexias

    1. Reading problems. There is no complete definition at this time.

        a. Congenital = Born with.

        b. Auditory = Cannot relate sounds to symbols.

        c. Visual = Cannot relate visual symbols.

        d. Global = No auditory, visual or kinesthetic cues reinforce symbol identification.

B. Dyscalculias = Math problems.

C. <u>Dysgraphias</u>　　　　= Writing problems interfering
　　　　　　　　　　　　with spelling and written
　　　　　　　　　　　　language.

D. <u>Perceptual Problems</u>
　　　　　　　　　　　　= Difficulty understanding
　　　　　　　　　　　　environmental stimuli the way
　　　　　　　　　　　　most people do.　The BRAIN
　　　　　　　　　　　　perceives in:

　　1.　Auditory　　　= Problems in understanding
　　　　　　　　　　　　sounds.　It is not an acuity
　　　　　　　　　　　　problem.　The auditory stimuli
　　　　　　　　　　　　is correctly received, but not
　　　　　　　　　　　　interpreted correctly by the
　　　　　　　　　　　　brain centers.

　　　　a. Figure-ground
　　　　　　　　　　　　= Being able to attend to audi-
　　　　　　　　　　　　tory stimuli and shut out the
　　　　　　　　　　　　unimportant.

　　　　b. Form-Constancy
　　　　　　　　　　　　= Being able to discriminate
　　　　　　　　　　　　words and sounds, understand
　　　　　　　　　　　　the different meanings of
　　　　　　　　　　　　"two," "too," or keep string of
　　　　　　　　　　　　words together to follow direc-
　　　　　　　　　　　　tions or understand communica-
　　　　　　　　　　　　tion.

　　　　c. Closure　　= Phonetic analysis of words,
　　　　　　　　　　　　anticipating word endings as in
　　　　　　　　　　　　grammar (ask, asked, asking,
　　　　　　　　　　　　etc.).

　　　　d. Memory　　= Being able to recall immediate
　　　　　　　　　　　　or long term sequential audi-
　　　　　　　　　　　　tory stimuli as in nursery
　　　　　　　　　　　　rhymes, counting or saying the
　　　　　　　　　　　　alphabet even though one may
　　　　　　　　　　　　not know the visual symbols for
　　　　　　　　　　　　these numerals and letters.

　　2.　Visual　　　= Problem in understanding the
　　　　　　　　　　　　visual symbols which are seen.
　　　　　　　　　　　　Not a visual acuity problem.
　　　　　　　　　　　　The visual stimuli is received
　　　　　　　　　　　　correctly, but not interpreted
　　　　　　　　　　　　correctly by the brain centers.

　　　　a. Visual-Motor
　　　　　　　　　　　　= Coordinating eye and hand
　　　　　　　　　　　　together to reproduce visual
　　　　　　　　　　　　interpretation of stimuli.

　　　　b. Figure-Ground
　　　　　　　　　　　　= Sorting foreground and back-
　　　　　　　　　　　　ground of intersecting stimuli.
　　　　　　　　　　　　Depth perception.

c. Form Constancy
   = Discrimination of similar forms
   -circles-ovals-squares-
   rectangles, etc.

d. Position In Space
   = Recognizing directionality,
   right-left, in front-behind,
   up-down.

e. Spatial Relations
   = (Stereo) -- The ability to see
   things in relationship to each
   other, that a cube has six
   sides with one on top, one on
   bottom, one right, one on the
   left, one in front and one in
   back and that all the sides
   are dependent on each other.

E. Motor Problems   = Difficulty interpreting
                       environment through body
                       movements and contacts.

1. Body Image   = How we psychologically see
                       ourselves.

2. Body Schema   = Use of body in space, know
                       where the chair is and how to
                       sit down without looking, how
                       to scratch and itch where we
                       can't see, maintain balance in
                       walking, running, sitting, etc.
                       without looking.

3. Gross Motor Coordination
                     = Balance, large body movements
                       such as are used in walking,
                       running, jumping, hopping, etc.

4. Fine Motor Coordination
                     = Aiming, catching, kicking,
                       handwriting, sewing, manipula-
                       ting (puzzles, turning pages
                       of a book).

Auditory Discrimination Test (Wepman)

Form 1

		X	Y			X	Y
1.	tub - tug			21.	cat - cap		
2.	lack - lack			22.	din - bin		
3.	web - wed			23.	lath - lash		
4.	leg - led			24.	bum - bomb		
5.	chap - chap			25.	clothe - clove		
6.	gum - dumb			26.	moon - noon		
7.	bale - gale			27.	shack - sack		
8.	sought - fought			28.	sheaf - sheath		
9.	vow - thou			29.	king - king		
10.	shake - shape			30.	badge - badge		
11.	zest - zest			31.	pork - cork		
12.	wretch - wretch			32.	fie - thigh		
13.	thread - shred			33.	shoal - shawl		
14.	jam - jam			34.	tall - tall		
15.	bass - bath			35.	par - par		
16.	tin - pin			36.	pat - pat		
17.	pat - pack			37.	muff - muss		
18.	dim - din			38.	pose - pose		
19.	coast - toast			39.	lease - leash		
20.	thimble - symbol			40.	pen - pin		

ERROR SCORE

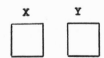

X   Y

Word Recognition Test for Children with Dyslexia

PRE-PRIMER
all_____
blue_____
come_____
get_____
have_____
house_____
little_____
play_____
ride_____
want_____
see_____
saw_____

PRIMER
boat_____
but_____
duck_____
shine_____
kitten_____
like_____
now_____
are_____
put_____
saw_____
stop_____
think_____

FIRST GRADE
about_____
color_____
course_____
live_____
met_____
paint_____
street_____
tree_____
walk_____

SECOND GRADE
cross_____
best_____
burn_____
care_____
fire_____
gone_____
new_____
off_____
pig_____
write_____
shell_____
today_____
hide_____
kept_____
wheel_____

THIRD GRADE
block_____
daddy_____
lit_____
mind_____
north_____
rich_____
signal_____
swing_____
trail_____
wall_____
beech_____
chance_____
cottage_____
fog_____
scared_____

FOURTH GRADE
lush_____
firmly_____
hungry_____
loyal_____
oven_____
pond_____
sauce_____
truck_____

FIFTH GRADE
hobby_____
chart_____
embarrass_____
surroundings_____

SIXTH GRADE
abbey_____
fur_____
grammar_____
isolate_____
loving_____
outstanding_____
suspicious_____

JUNIOR HIGH
bait_____
armament_____
blunt_____
devoted_____
loveliness_____
outstretched_____
poorly_____

SENIOR HIGH
abandon_____
detestible_____
graduation_____
lovable_____
recital_____
snuggle_____

Simple Movement Test

Name_____

Date Tested_____

Date/Birth_____ Age_____

Level of Cooperation_____

General Appearance_____

FOLLOWING DIRECTIONS ON SUBJECT

1.	Show me your left hand	Cor.	Incor.
2.	Show me your right leg	Cor.	Incor.
3.	Show me your left eye	Cor.	Incor.
4.	Show me your right ear	Cor.	Incor.
5.	Show me your left leg	Cor.	Incor.
6.	Show me your right hand	Cor.	Incor.

Consistent   #Cor.   #Incor.

ON EXAMINER

1.	Show me my left ear	Cor.	Incor.
2.	Show me my right eye	Cor.	Incor.
3.	Show me my left hand	Cor.	Incor.
4.	Show me my right knee	Cor.	Incor.

Consistent   #Cor.   #Incor.

CROSSING THE MID-LINE 2 PART COMMAND

1.	Cross your left leg over your right knee	Cor.	Incor.
2.	Touch your left elbow with your right hand	Cor.	Incor.
3.	Touch your right ear with your left hand	Cor.	Incor.
4.	Touch your left foot with your right hand	Cor.	Incor.
5.	Touch your right knee with your left hand	Cor.	Incor.

Consistent   #Cor.   #Incor.

Consistent Total			#Cor.	#Incor.

Optokinetic Eye Movements	N.	Abn.

Face-Hand Test	Eyes Closed		Eyes Open	
	G	P	G	P

Sound-Touch Test	Eyes Closed		Eyes Open	
	G	P	G	P

Position Sense	Good	Fair	Poor

RAPID LIP MOVEMENTS	G	F	P

Point Discrimination
Good   Poor

Visual Figure Groun
Good   Fair   Poor

Tactile Figure Writing
Good   Fair   Poor

MOTOR EXAMINATION

Demonstrate each item

		G	F	P
1.	Stand on right foot (5 sec.)	G	F	P
2.	Stand on left foot (5 sec.)	G	F	P
3.	Tapping right foot	G	F	P
4.	Associated Body Movements	G	F	P
5.	Tapping left foot	G	F	P
6.	Associated body movements	G	F	P
7.	Hop on right foot (5 sec.)	G	F	P
8.	Hop on left foot (5 sec.)	G	F	P
9.	Standing heel to toe (5 sec.)	G	F	P
10.	Walking straight line (6 feet)	G	F	P
11.	Walking straight line eyes closed	G	F	P
12.	Walking backwards	G	F	P
13.	Tapping foot & finger (right)	G	F	P
14.	Tapping foot & finger (left)	G	F	P
15.	Touch finger-nose (right)	G	F	P
16.	Touch finger-nose (left)	G	F	P
17.	Rapid finger movements (right)	G	F	P
18.	Rapid finger movements (left)	G	F	P

144

Audiogram

Name_____   Date_____

Address_____   Age_____
                                      By_____

```
125 500   2000    4000    8000
  250 1000    3000    6000
```

*Difference in dB (ASA (VS. ISO)

9 15 14 10 8.5 8.5 6.0 9.5 11.5

Graph with vertical axis: -10, 0, 10, 20, 30, 40, 50, 60, 70, 80, 90, 100, 110

( ) ISO-64 Reference thresholds
( ) ASA-51 Reference thresholds
*Add Difference in dB to ASA
values to obtain ISO values.

	Right	Left
TEST Ear		Ear
	(Red)	(Blue)
//// ////		//////
Air	0-0	X-X
Bone		

Speech reception
Threshold

R................db

L................db

Bin Ph...........db

Bin FF...........db

Speech disc.

.....db   R......%

.....db   L......%

.....Bin   Ph.....%

.....Bin   F.F....%

Testing Conditions

Noisy
Adequate
Good

1. When has your child had a hearing problem?

2. What are the medical reasons?

3. Who had had hearing problems in the family?

4. Does anyone complain that your child does not
   seem to hear?

5. Describe place, time and behavior when child
   does not hear?

Bender-Gestalt Scoring Sheet

(For Children ages 5 to 10 years)

Name_____   Date_____

Time: Finish_____   R.Hand_____   Comments:_____

       Start_____   L.Hand_____   _____

       Total_____   _____

Fig. A

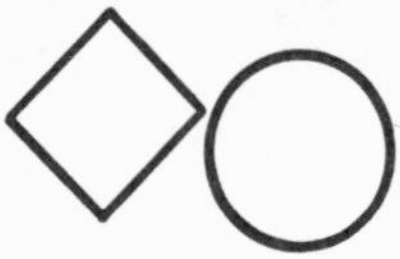

1a   Distortion of shape   _____
1b   Disproportion   _____
2   Rotation   _____
3   Integration   _____

Fig. 1

4   Circles for dots   _____
5   Rotation   _____
6   Perseveration   _____

Fig. 2

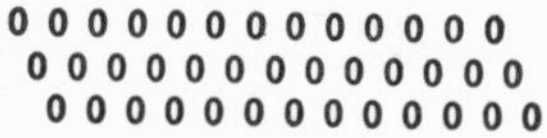

7   Rotation   _____
8   Raw added, omitted   _____
9   Perseveration   _____

Fig. 3

10   Circles for dots   _____
11   Rotation   _____
12a   Shape lost   _____
12b   Lines for dots   _____

Fig. 4

13   Rotation   _____
14   Integration   _____

Fig. 5

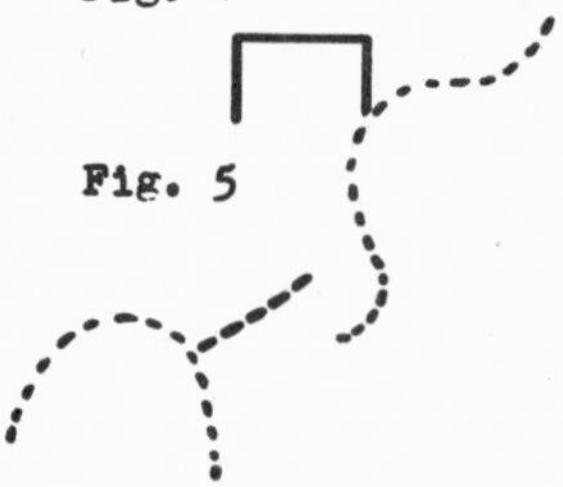

15   Circles for dots   _____
16   Rotation   _____
17a   Shape lost   _____
17b   Lines for dots   _____

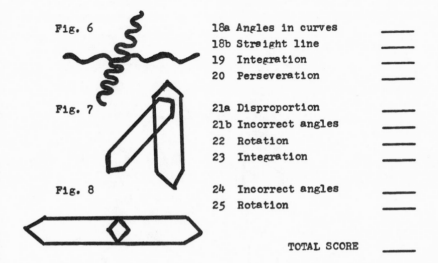

Fig. 6

Fig. 7

Fig. 8

18a Angles in curves _____
18b Straight line _____
19 Integration _____
20 Perseveration _____

21a Disproportion _____
21b Incorrect angles _____
22 Rotation _____
23 Integration _____

24 Incorrect angles _____
25 Rotation _____

TOTAL SCORE _____

Pre-School Form Test

(for those children too young for Bender-Gestalt)

Name_____

Age_____ Date_____

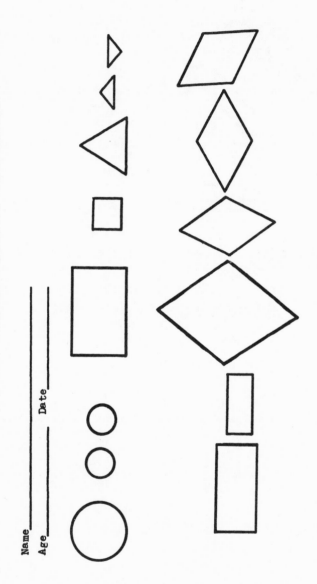

Index

149

1 2 3 4 5 6 7 ← P Y → 9 8 7 6 5 4